Henry Wilder Foote

The commemoration by King's chapel

Boston

Henry Wilder Foote

The commemoration by King's chapel
Boston

ISBN/EAN: 9783337113469

Printed in Europe, USA, Canada, Australia, Japan

Cover: Foto ©ninafisch / pixelio.de

More available books at **www.hansebooks.com**

WITH THE COMPLIMENTS

OF

𝔗𝔥𝔢 𝔐𝔦𝔫𝔦𝔰𝔱𝔢𝔯, 𝔚𝔞𝔯𝔡𝔢𝔫𝔰, 𝔞𝔫𝔡 𝔙𝔢𝔰𝔱𝔯𝔶

OF

KING'S CHAPEL, BOSTON.

EXTERIOR OF KING'S CHAPEL, Dec. 15, 1886.

THE COMMEMORATION

BY

KING'S CHAPEL, BOSTON,

OF THE

Completion of Two Hundred Years

SINCE ITS FOUNDATION,

ON WEDNESDAY, DECEMBER 15, 1886.

ALSO

THREE HISTORICAL SERMONS.

WITH ILLUSTRATIONS.

BOSTON:
LITTLE, BROWN, AND COMPANY.
1887.

University Press:
JOHN WILSON AND SON, CAMBRIDGE.

INTRODUCTORY NOTE.

THE decorations employed in the celebration are in part reproduced in the illustrations of this volume. They are partly taken from the Rev. Mr. Foote's "Annals of King's Chapel;" while for the portraits the Committee are also indebted to the courtesy of Messrs. Ticknor and Company, publishers of the "Memorial History of Boston;" to the owners of those which have been specially photographed for this volume; and to Messrs. Houghton, Mifflin, and Company, and to Mr. Justin Winsor, publishers and editor of the "Narrative and Critical History of America," for permission to use that of Lieutenant-Governor Dummer from the fifth volume of that work. The drawing of the exterior arrangement of flags is made by Mr. J. TEMPLEMAN COOLIDGE, 3d, for this volume. The cut on page 2, representing the church when it was approached by several steps, before Tremont Street had been filled in to a uniform level, and before the balustrade on the roof had been removed, is enlarged from one by Abel Bowen about 1833. The die on the cover is copied from one impressed on "Bridgman's King's Chapel Epitaphs," and is taken from a picture painted for the Rev. Mr. Greenwood about 1830. It shows not only the church but the burial-ground as it then appeared, before a desecrating hand had removed the gravestones from the graves to which they belonged.

BOSTON, March, 1887.

CONTENTS.

Preliminary Proceedings.

	PAGE
ACTION OF THE PROPRIETORS OF KING'S CHAPEL	3
COMMITTEE APPOINTED BY THE WARDENS AND VESTRY OF KING'S CHAPEL	3
REPORT OF COMMITTEE	4
COMMITTEES APPOINTED	6
INVITATIONS AND ARRANGEMENTS	6

Historical Sermons.

| REV. HENRY WILDER FOOTE, PREACHED DEC. 5, 1886 | 11 |
| " " " " PREACHED DEC. 12, 1886 | 34 |

Commemorative Services.

PROGRAMME	53
COMMEMORATIVE SERVICES	69
ADDRESS OF WELCOME, BY WILLIAM MINOT, ESQ.	75
RELIGIOUS SERVICES	76

CONTENTS.

	PAGE
ADDRESS OF THE MINISTER	80
„ „ GOVERNOR ROBINSON	89
„ „ REV. GEORGE EDWARD ELLIS, D.D., LL.D.	96
„ „ REV. GEORGE A. GORDON	105
„ „ PRESIDENT CHARLES WILLIAM ELIOT, LL.D.	109
„ „ REV. PHILLIPS BROOKS, D.D.	112
„ „ REV. JOHN HOPKINS MORISON, D.D.	122
ADDRESS AND POEM BY REV. JAMES FREEMAN CLARKE, D.D.	128
POEM BY OLIVER WENDELL HOLMES, M.D., LL.D. D.C.L.	131
ADDRESS OF PROF. ANDREW PRESTON PEABODY, D.D., LL.D.	134
ADDRESS OF PROF. FRANCIS GREENWOOD PEABODY	138

Correspondence.

FROM OFFICIAL PERSONS AND OTHER INVITED GUESTS	145
FROM DESCENDANTS OF THE CHURCH	148
FROM CLERGYMEN	154

Closing Sermon.

REV. HENRY WILDER FOOTE, PREACHED DEC. 19, 1886	167

INDEX	193

ILLUSTRATIONS.

	PAGE
Exterior of the Church, 1886	*Frontispiece*
King's Chapel in 1833	2
Card of Invitation	6
Royal Arms	7
Interior of the Church, 1886	8
Earliest King's Chapel, 1687	53
First Page of the Earliest Record Book	54
Pulpit, 1717	55
Autograph of Rev. Robert Ratcliffe	63
Facsimile of Flags in Exterior Decoration	69
Escutcheons used in the Decoration	71
Portrait of Governor Joseph Dudley	86
,, ,, Mrs. Rebecca (Tyng) Dudley	98
,, ,, Governor William Burnet	110
,, ,, Governor Jonathan Belcher	122
,, ,, Lieut.-Governor William Dummer	130
,, ,, Governor Thomas Pownall	146
,, ,, Governor Thomas Hutchinson	158
,, ,, Peter Faneuil, Esquire	170
,, ,, Rev. James Freeman	182

PRELIMINARY PROCEEDINGS.

KING'S CHAPEL IN 1833.

PRELIMINARY PROCEEDINGS.

AT the annual meeting of the Proprietors of King's Chapel in Boston, held April 26, 1886, the Senior Warden, ARTHUR T. LYMAN, Esq., laid before the meeting a communication from the Minister in relation to having appropriate notice taken of the 15th June, as the two hundredth anniversary of the organization of this church, by putting up a memorial thereof, or otherwise. The subject was referred to the Wardens and Vestry, with full powers.

At a meeting of the Wardens and Vestry, May 2, 1886, the following gentlemen were appointed a Committee to take action in regard to such anniversary:

WILLIAM PERKINS.	GREELY S. CURTIS.
JOHN REVERE.	PATRICK T. JACKSON.
GEORGE HIGGINSON.	J. RANDOLPH COOLIDGE, JR.

This Committee subsequently reported, at the meeting of the Wardens and Vestry, held Nov. 18, 1886, as follows : —

REPORT.

The Wardens and Vestry having appointed a committee to report to them a plan for the proper Commemoration of the Two Hundredth Year of Church Life of King's Chapel, — which was founded June 15, 1686, and celebrated its first communion service on the second Sabbath of August, 1686, — the following is proposed : —

It having been impracticable in the midsummer season of general dispersion to gather our whole congregation for a service which is of universal interest to them, it was thought best to defer the Commemoration until this time. It is now recommended that Wednesday, December 15, be fixed as the day for such a service, and that these arrangements be made for its fit observance : —

1. A committee of the Vestry, increased by a number of young and active members of the congregation, to carry out the necessary details.

2. Invitations to be sent to all persons now or formerly connected with the church, so far as they can be ascertained ; to ministers of the older churches and leading persons in the city ; and to such others as may be deemed best.

3. The service to consist of special music by a large choir, and of addresses by the following persons : —

The GOVERNOR, as the successor of eight Royal Governors who worshipped here ;

The following persons who were born into and brought up in King's Chapel, namely : —

    THE PRESIDENT OF HARVARD COLLEGE ;
    Rev. DR. JAMES FREEMAN CLARKE ;
    Rev. FRANCIS GREENWOOD PEABODY ;
    Rev. Dr. FARLEY, of Brooklyn, N. Y. ;
    Rev. Dr. THAYER, of Newport, R. I. ; and others ;

Members of the present congregation; as Rev. Dr. PEABODY and Dr. OLIVER WENDELL HOLMES;

The MINISTER of the OLD SOUTH CHURCH, in remembrance of its special connection with our history;

A REPRESENTATIVE of the EPISCOPAL CHURCH, of which King's Chapel was the mother-church in New England.

4. It is also recommended that some social meeting for the evening of the same day be arranged for, if practicable.

5. To perpetuate the remembrance of this historic occasion, it is recommended that a design be obtained, and a bronze or marble tablet or monument placed in the church, marking the special connection of King's Chapel with the early history of this country, and recording some of the names of those associated with the parish in its pre-Revolutionary history.

For the Committee.
WILLIAM PERKINS,
Chairman.

The Wardens and Vestry accordingly

"*Voted*, That Rev. HENRY W. FOOTE be added to the original Committee; and that the Committee be authorized to increase their number to sixteen by the addition of gentlemen connected with the parish, — the Committee so enlarged to be empowered to make all the arrangements necessary for the proper celebration, on Wednesday the fifteenth day of December, on the completion of two hundred years since the foundation of this parish; and that they are also authorized, if deemed expedient, to prepare a Memorial Volume, containing the addresses made at the celebration, and other historic matters connected therewith."

The Committee proceeded accordingly to add to their number the following gentlemen:

J. Templeman Coolidge, 3d.
Edward S. Grew.
Thomas B. Hall.
Horace A. Lamb.
A. Lawrence Lowell.

Francis C. Lowell.
George R. Minot.
Thomas Minns.
Charles E. Sampson.
Roger Wolcott.

They also appointed the following Sub-Committees, namely: —

On Speakers and Order of Exercises.

Henry W. Foote.   Greely S. Curtis.
          A. Lawrence Lowell.

On Music and Decorations.

J. Randolph Coolidge, Jr.   Greely S. Curtis.
J. Templeman Coolidge, 3d.   Horace A. Lamb.
          George R. Minot.

On Invitations, Tickets, and Printing.

Thomas B. Hall.   Thomas Minns.
Francis C. Lowell.   Roger Wolcott.
          Henry W. Foote.

On Expenses.

George Higginson.   Edward S. Grew.
          Charles E. Sampson.

On Memorial Volume.

Henry W. Foote.   Patrick T. Jackson.
          Thomas Minns.

Invitations to the Commemoration were extended to a large number of ministers of the older churches in Massachusetts of different denominations; to ministers of churches deriving their descent from King's Chapel before

1686   1886

King's Chapel, Boston.

Cordially invites

to attend the services in commemoration of the completion of

Two Hundred Years

Wednesday, December 15th at 2 o'clock, P.M.

William Perkins   Committee
Thomas B. Hall   on
James C. Lowell   Invitations
Roger Wolcott

Arthur T. Lyman   Wardens
Charles P. Curtis

the American Revolution, and to other clergymen of the Protestant Episcopal Church in Massachusetts and elsewhere; to various bishops and ministers, Protestant and Roman Catholic; to the Governor, Lieutenant-Governor, and other officials of the Commonwealth of Massachusetts; to the Mayor of Boston, and many other prominent citizens; to the Right Reverend the Lord Bishop of London, and, as far as they could be ascertained, to representatives in this generation of families formerly belonging to the parish, and to others who themselves have been at any time connected with it.

Admission to the church was necessarily by ticket only; and it was filled to its fullest capacity through the whole of the services.

(Formerly hung over the door of the Province House.)

INTERIOR OF KING'S CHAPEL, Dec. 15, 1886.

HISTORICAL SERMONS

ON THE OCCASION OF THE

Completion of Two Hundred Years

SINCE THE FOUNDATION OF

KING'S CHAPEL, BOSTON.

BY REV. HENRY WILDER FOOTE.

HISTORICAL SERMONS.

I.

THUS SAITH THE LORD GOD: I WILL ALSO TAKE OF THE HIGHEST BRANCH OF THE HIGH CEDAR, AND WILL SET IT; I WILL CROP OFF FROM THE TOP OF HIS YOUNG TWIGS A TENDER ONE, AND WILL PLANT IT UPON AN HIGH MOUNTAIN AND EMINENT: IN THE MOUNTAIN OF THE HEIGHT OF ISRAEL WILL I PLANT IT; IT SHALL BRING FORTH BOUGHS, AND BEAR FRUIT, AND BE A GOODLY CEDAR. — *Ezekiel*, xvii. 22, 23.

ON Wednesday, the 15th of this month, we shall mark with fitting celebration the fact that this is the two hundredth year since the beginning of this church. It is not, indeed, the day itself in the year; for the proper foundation time of the church fell in that fair season of the twelvemonth when, in 1686, men found Boston a pleasant place by the water-side to abide in, — as now they find it a place to flee from; as when the First Church, the mother of all the religious life of this good city, six years ago kept its two hundred and fiftieth anniversary, its minister had to say: "We can plead as apologies for our delay only those habits of modern life, even in our Northern city, which make a midsummer gathering all but impossible." There are, indeed, several birthdays for us in that year 1686, — according as we mark the day when the first religious service of the infant congregation was held, May 20; or that of the first meeting for organization, June 15; or July 4, when that organization was completed, by a strange coincidence anticipating the birthday of America; or the 2d of August, which I like best to think of as the true foundation day of the church, the day when the first celebration of the Lord's Supper was held, according to the reverend usage which was preparing a home for itself here among the Puritan community.

The great festival of our College has lately reminded us of the plain yet heroic beginnings out of which New England sprang. The history of the beginnings of this ancient church brings to remembrance another chapter of the annals of our country, equally worthy to be kept from oblivion, it seems to me, and which interweaves, like a thread of gold in cloth of sober russet, elements of light and color and warmth in the narrative which had long been a stranger to them, as it brings the great power and presence of England, our mother-country, into visible authority in this Colony of Massachusetts Bay.

The recent years have been thickly studded with commemorations of the foundation of successive churches and towns in this old commonwealth, which filled the eventful years from 1620 to 1640. In them all, it is always the Puritan idea and the Puritan founders that are brought into fresh and deserved honor. King's Chapel stands alone in that first century, in setting forth another side of the story, — a side historical and of deep religious significance, as well as most picturesque in its contrasts. Yet we shall best be able to understand this if we try first of all to put ourselves into understanding and sympathetic relations with the conditions of the community where our church planted itself two centuries ago.

The great corner-stone on which the New England polity rested, — and still rests, — is the thought that *God rules*. Not only that He has ruled in the past, that He made the world, or that He saved the world, but that He is so intensely present that all things in the comparison with Him verily cease to exist. It is the faith that He is the God of the moral world not less than of the physical world, a legislator of whom it is not less true that His laws can be understood and applied by men than it is that the forces of Nature silently do His will, — with the difference that His children can serve Him intelligently, "hearkening unto the voice of His word." In this faith, with its double consequence concerning the individual and concerning government, lies wrapped up the history of New England, — that is to say, really, the history of America. It may fitly be called a religious history; it is a story possessed by the conviction of the Ruling God. It stands before posterity to speak for itself by the type of character which it moulded, by the strength of faith through which it wrought, by its works for men and for God.

Those fathers of New England justify the claim which is made for them on our pride and loyalty, by the great ideas which they left to their posterity as seed-grain for the world's great harvest of faith and hope. In the days when the first James and Charles were harrying them out of England, they sought beyond the sea to embody their mighty vision, — the ideal of a Christian Commonwealth, in which God should be King and Judge; and although they erred in trying to follow too literally the antique pattern, and could not well see how to gain the spirit without literal copying of the letter, the Living Spirit of the Living God had descended mightily upon them and possessed them, so that they "builded better than they knew." Not caring to be rich, or wise, or famous, if only they might serve the Lord with a pure and acceptable worship, "all these things were added unto them" and to their children. Grand and honored forms of the past, they stand forth from the shadows that have closed around and hide so much from us, — the founders of a new age. Quaint-garbed fathers of the New England of to-day, in doublet and cloak, with steeple-crowned hat and solemn mien, we can easily seem to see them once more walking the streets of the little town, as citizens of another country, "even an heavenly," and dwellers in "a city whose founder and builder is God."

Even their children cannot claim that the Puritans were perfect men; and they themselves would be farthest from claiming it. But they were colossal,

— not smooth men, but scarred and weather-beaten by great encounters with enemies seen and unseen. "Paint me," said Cromwell to Sir Peter Lely, "as I am;" and the very warts on that heroic face were set down on the canvas for posterity to look upon. The Puritan can well afford to be painted as he was. He who was so severe with himself could be very rigid with others also. He found his conscience a hard master, — the penances it imposed often more grievous than hair shirts or flagellations; and if his conscience burdened him, it did not seem unfitting that it should rule others also with a rod of iron. Such men as these would have found us difficult to tolerate, and we should probably have shrunk from before their terrible presence.

Never, surely, did men take in hand so bold a work, — say, rather, so trustful a work, — as did that first generation of Englishmen here, of whom "according to the flesh" our ancestors, their children, came. To us what they did looks so venerable, — its success is so vindicated by its issues, — that we often fail to realize the greatness of soul, the supreme faith in the Invisible God of Righteousness, which was needed to go behind the triple wall of form and court and established church, with its ritual and authority, to the wells of living water in the Scripture and to the present help of the Lord of Hosts. They aimed to build their tabernacle "in all things after the pattern showed them in the mount;" and if they sometimes followed Moses rather than Christ, the Eternal Spirit who also spake to Moses was able to outlast the Old Testament in their dispensation, and to prepare the way for the coming of the New.

It is often, in these days, made a reproach to the Puritans that they wanted none here of any way of thinking save their own, — as if they had set up to be the fathers of what Roger Williams calls "soul-liberty," and then had deserted their principle. But they neither sought nor claimed nor desired what is called liberty of thought, in the modern sense of the word. They had come hither, at the cost of infinite peril and hardship, to escape from earthly masters, but not at all in order that they might be left free to their own devices. They sought liberty from the earthly masters only that they might freely give up to the Heavenly their own wills, — yea, their own minds, acknowledging God as having eminent domain over all. They believed that they had in the Scriptures such a revelation from Him that they could safely appeal to that infallible Law for direction in the minutest particulars of life, and in the greatest; nor was there any difference to them between one part and another part, but all were equally binding, — the regulations of Leviticus, as much as the precepts of Christ.

The world has since attained a wiser conception than theirs of the inspiration of the Holy Book; we have a more spiritual insight into its true meaning, and a better discrimination between its various parts. But we may well ask ourselves the very searching question, whether we have as living a conviction of the Living God present with us, searching, knowing, upholding us, as they had, — whether we find it as natural to turn to Him for light and strength as they did. We may deem them illogical, shutting up the Divine Being as they did within the contents of the Book of Books, and yet combining with this even Bibliolatry such intense faith in the God who is the Father of our spirits, "God over all, blessed forever." Nevertheless, this they did; and in bequeathing to their children this supreme trust, they left us the truth of truths, the mightiest of inspirations and powers whether for our personal or our national life. And being willing to submit themselves to this Divine code of laws, in which they believed that the Ruler of the universe had given them "a sufficient rule of faith and practice," they expected others who came after them to this bleak corner of the world to do likewise.

A religion so intensely earnest, so severely simple, must needs have fashioned for itself an outward order quite other than that of the mother-church and the mother-land which these men had left, — shaped by it only by reaction. We are in part familiar with this in the congregational order of ritual to-day, yet only in a softened guise, and with many adornments on which the primitive founders would have looked darkly. What, then, was that form of worship which that early generation of Boston Puritans had wrought out for themselves, — not wholly like any other? Let me quote the sympathetic description of it by the Rev. Dr. Rufus Ellis: —

"The little congregation had no need to fashion any ritual. They found it only too delicious to pray as the Spirit gave them utterance. They will not have even the Bible read in the course of their worship, unless it is expounded, and the truths brought into the light by the Divine blessing upon a living ministry. They will have none of what they called 'dumb reading.'

"What were styled 'conceived,' or as we say *ex tempore*, prayers had been allowed them in their old church only grudgingly and in very stinted measure. Here there shall be no other prayers, — not though it were the Lord's Prayer, which had been so misused as a *pater noster* and by vain repetitions. They would have no white surplice with Romish priests, but would minister in the scholar's black gown of Geneva. It seemed to them a mere formality, and too much like the genuflections of the old superstition, to bow the head at the name of Jesus, though none could exceed them in their reverence for that Holy One. Like the early disciples, they would gather about the sacramental table rather than kneel about the altar, lest haply men should say, 'they worship the bread and the wine.' They will have no funeral prayers, but will bear their dead to the last resting-place and lay them away in touching silence, lest they should be thought to pray for the departed spirit and say masses in the ancient manner. They will not only lay aside the marriage ring as heathenish, but by a strange revulsion they will have marriage a civil service, to be performed, not by the minister, but by a magistrate. They cannot quite refuse to sing, — but there shall be no instrument save the human voice, and such rough psalmody as was supplied to the Puritans of Amsterdam by Henry Ainsworth; their tunes, some ten in number, oftenest York, Hackney, Windsor, St. Mary, and St. Martyn's."

Such was the type of worship which the God-fearing Puritans had elaborated in this far corner of the world. Meantime, great events had swept over the Old World which they had left. Charles I. had died upon the block, to answer for the oppressions which drove them forth. The Commonwealth of England had risen and fallen. The son of Charles Stuart was back upon the throne, with no love in his heart for the men in England or here who had done that work upon his father.

Meantime, the generation had gone of those who knew the Old England, — Winthrop, Thomas Dudley, Wilson, Cotton, — some of the noblest of the earth; and fifty years had hardened this primitive community into fixed conditions.

That people we can easily picture to ourselves, from the abundant though not over friendly descriptions which have survived from the pens of not very sympathetic visitors to this distant shore. Indeed, I cannot but think that we their descendants have enough of them surviving in us to make it easier, one would suppose, than it sometimes seems to be, to reproduce their likeness out of our own consciousness. A fixed and resolute race, — the English iron tempered to steel by the struggle with the untamed nature of the wilderness, the hardships of the first fifty years of life here before the climate was understood, the rugged world civilized and softened, the comforts of fireside and food fairly won. The law of the "survival of the fittest" had worked with all its merciless severity, and left only the toughest in body and mind, — those who would not yield to the New England winter, and were not likely to yield one jot beyond necessity to Old England's dictation. A religious Emigration, they carried in themselves the seeds of a sacred contentiousness, which contained the germs, though long repressed, of the sects which have enriched our annals with more varieties of Protestantism than Bossuet included in his great work on that subject.

Already, in the first generation, the vision of absolute religious unity was rudely dispelled by the sharp strifes evoked by Mrs. Hutchinson, the earliest representative of Women's Rights; and Rhode Island was found a much needed and salutary safety-valve for the explosive ecclesiastical elements. Roger Williams and Gorton were free at that distance to work out their theories, but could come no nearer to mar the peace of Israel. The second generation saw multiplying elements of discord, — the Quaker, shrieking denunciations of the "priests of Baal" in the steeple-houses, lashed to the cart's tail, hung from the Boston Elm; the Baptist, breaking the ice of strong hostility to administer the waters, his saving ordinance. Nor was there perfect harmony within the bosom of the churches themselves. The Second Church, which was afterwards illuminated by the ministry of the Mathers, — father, son, and grandson, — had indeed grown peacefully out of the First Church. But the Third, which we call the Old South, was the monument of a bitter strife — the controversy which convulsed the whole colony for years — concerning the proper subjects for infant baptism.

On one point, however, the elements most mutually hostile were agreed, — that is, in their feeling of dislike and fear of the Church of England. Much as they might be opposed to each other, the widest fissure between them was not so deep but that it would close up solidly if the faintest tremor of that approaching earthquake shook the ground. Randolph wrote to the Bishop of London, 1682: "There was a great difference between the old church and the members of the new church about baptisme, and their members joining in full communion with either church; this was soe high that there was imprisoning of parties and great disturbances; but now, heereing of my proposals for ministers to be sent over, . . . they are now joyned together, about a fortnight ago, and pray to God to confound the devices of all who disturbe their peace and liberties." Nor is this strange. The Episcopalian who wonders at it to-day is no more like the type which Randolph represented and which the Puritans hated and dreaded, than is the Quaker, who represents some of the gentlest and purest elements in our social life, like the wild figures clad in sackcloth, or in the less substantial garments of our first parents before the Fall, whose prophesyings were known by the same name. To every New Englander, the English Church stood for a spiritual tyranny which had driven the fathers out into the wilderness; in practice a corruption of the simplicity of the Scriptural rule; its hierarchy contrary to the gospel; its book of prayer idolatrous; its adherents a worldly element demoralizing to the best welfare of New England, — to be kept out if it could be done; if not, at least to be prohibited from practising their empty form of religionism on the Lord's day, and to be held under the watch and ward of the Congregational churches in hopes to regenerate them in a purer way. Nor was it only the ancient grievance against Archbishop Laud which smarted in memory. No one could tell how far, but they feared very far, the Church and State religion of Charles II. was identical in policy and principle with that of Charles I. They knew well what happened to Scotch Covenanters and to English Puritans, and had no reason for confidence in their own exemption from the same measure. Moreover, the English Church and the English State were identical. The representatives of the one would look after the interests of the other; and the tower of King's Chapel, if such a place should once be built, would be, with its gilt mitre and crown, a very short distance from the head of Long Wharf, with the royal flag flying above a custom-house. Those who are disturbed because the Massachusetts people liked their commercial independence better than paying duties as loyal subjects of Great Britain, forget that there may be an honest difference of opinion regarding the powers conferred by the charter of Charles I. As the Puritans viewed it, this was practically independence.

On that they had acted for fifty years; and only the force of the stronger could modify their action.

The point which the ruling influences here forgot, however, at the time which we are considering, was the very important fact that new elements had now come in among them, to a considerable degree modifying the tone if not *of* the community at least *in* the community. The American process had begun, which we see in our own day (and not wholly to our liking), by which there is perpetually going on a transfusion of alien manners, customs, ways of thought and life into the spirit of our people. Even in our own time the process, though inevitable, is not gracefully accepted by us. The New England fathers saw clearly enough that all this tended toward a profound modification, if not extinction, of the idea on which New England was founded. But the other elements were here to some extent, and they had come to stay,— Englishmen who felt that they had a right to come to an English colony, and who probably felt themselves better than the people whom they found here, from the very fact that they did not enjoy the type of religious ministrations which were dear to the New England heart. Lechford and Josselyn, a few years before, illustrate their state of mind. It did not make them more acceptable in the Puritan town that they had come to make money, and not for conscience' sake. But here they were, with clear preferences for the Church of England ritual in which they had been born and bred. They went to meeting, as the whole population did, and must, under law. But a sort of silent protest must have been felt in their presence, though they probably rarely ventured to show it as frankly as did Mrs. Randolph in 1682, when, sitting with her husband in Mr. Joyliffe's pew in the South Meeting-house, she was observed to "make a curtesy at the name of Jesus, even in prayer-time."

How many there were of this way of thinking it is impossible for us to discern through the mists of time. Randolph estimated the number of disaffected very high, — at four-fifths of the population; he also wrote home to the Bishop of London, after the Church of England had been set up here, that there was a congregation of four hundred. But his figures on all subjects are untrustworthy, unless we can check them from other sources of information; nor does he say how large a proportion was composed of "boys and negros," who until the Revolution constituted so large a part of the congregation of King's Chapel as to require a special officer to "look after" them, and whose "looking after" doubtless required pretty energetic measures of repression, — not very godly or profitable worshippers. The Records of King's Chapel contain no clear indication of the numbers of the congregation; I judge from them, however, that at first only a few persons of influence were willing to risk the obnoxious step of identifying themselves with the planting of the English Church here. Under the sunshine of Sir Edmund Andros the church blossomed into prosperity, but at his downfall the Puritans exulted in the thought that it had withered to the root.

These then were the elements that awaited the loss of the charter which befell at last in October, 1684, after nearly twenty years' threatening, — on one side agonized fear, on the other eager hope, that a spiritual domination, which was according to the point of the view beneficent or blasting, would be overthrown. The central figure in all this commotion is, of course, Edward Randolph.

Two years before the charter was annulled, and four years before the arrival here of the Rev. Robert Ratcliffe the first Church of England minister, Randolph had written to the Bishop of London, reminding him that "In my attendance on your lordship, I often exprest that some able ministers might be appoynted to performe the officies of the church with us. The main obstacle was (as might be supposed) how they should be maintayned."

Before any question of the mode of his support was settled, the minister himself arrived, — a long delayed blessing, — May 15, 1686. Nearly four years before, Randolph had written to the Bishop, "The very report [that your lordship hath remembered us and sent over a minister] hath given great satisfaction to many hundreds whose children are not baptized, and to as many who never, since they came out of England, received the sacraments." The cause of the delay till a year and a half after the charter was annulled, was the death of Charles II. and the changes consequent thereon.

Mr. Ratcliffe came in the "Rose" frigate, with Captain George, the same officer who was captured by the people in the memorable rising against Andros in April, 1689, and the same ship which they compelled to surrender on that great day. They brought with them the commission to Joseph Dudley as President of Massachusetts, Maine, Nova Scotia, and the lands between.

And now we approach the place which is destined to be the first cradle of our infant church, and the town-house of Boston becomes the scene of eventful things. We can look over Sewall's shoulder as he writes in his little brown diary day by day, and can enter into the intense though suppressed feeling of the writer at the events which brought home to all the reality of the change which had come. We see Randolph hurrying up from Nantasket on the arrival of the "Rose" on Friday, May 14, so that he reaches town by 8 A. M., and posting by coach to Roxbury to notify Major Dudley of his new dignity. We see the dignitaries whom Dudley has summoned to Captain Paige's, assuring their own eyes that it is really so, as they see "the Exemplification of the judgment against the Charter, with the Broad Seal affixed," and that it is hopeless to resist. The Sabbath intervenes, — a dark day for the New Englanders. Randolph and his family sit meekly in a pew at the South Meeting-house, and hear Mr. Willard pray, "not for the Governor or Government as formerly, but speak so as implies it to be changed or changing." On Monday the General Court sits at the town-house to hear their fate. "The Old Government," writes Sewall, " draws to the north side; Mr. Addington, Captain Smith, and I sit at the Table, there not being room; Major Dudley the President, Major Pynchon, Captain Gedney, Mr. Mason, Mr. Randolph, Captain Winthrop, Mr. Wharton, come in on the Left — Mr. Stoughton I left out. Came also Captain [of] King's Frigate, Gov! Hinkley, Gov! West, and sate on the Bench; and the Room pretty well filled with Spectators in an instant. Major Dudley made a Speech, that was sorry could treat them no longer as Government Company; Produced the Exemplification of the Charter's Condemnation, the Commission under the Broad Seal of England — both, . . . openly exhibiting them to the People; when had done, Deputy Governor said suppos'd they expected not the Court's Answer now, which the President took up and said they could not acknowledge them as such, and could no way capitulate with them; to which I think no Reply. When gone . . . spake our Minds. I chose to say after the Major Generall, adding that the foundations being destroyed, what can the Righteous do, — speaking against a Protest, which some spake for."

The dramatic close of this episode falls on the Friday following, when Sewall found the magistrates and deputies not at the town-house, but at the Governor's. "Mr. Nowell prayed that God would pardon each Magistrate and Deputy's Sin. Thanked God for our hithertos of Mercy fifty-six years, in which time sad calamities elsewhere, as Massacre Piedmont; thanked God for what we might expect from sundry of those now set over us. I moved to sing, so sung the 17th and 18th verses of Habakkuk." That touching and sublime expression of trust, which declares that "although the fig-tree shall not blossom, and the laborer of the olive shall fail, . . . yet I will rejoice in the Lord," was the expiring cry of the old New England theocracy. No wonder that as they saw the edifice of the fathers go down in ruins, "Many Tears were shed in Prayer and parting." Yet they expired with faith upon their lips.

But while the old glory thus withdrew its vanishing skirts from the noteworthy building which had seen the Government of Massachusetts administered under the charter by able and resolute lovers of the old New England way, the echoes of unfamiliar sounds in this Puritan air had already been heard within those walls; for on the Tuesday of that week, by whose authority we are not told, " Prayer was had at the Town House," — the first public administration of the English Church since the colony began. And the same day saw Mr. Ratcliffe marry a couple "according to the Service Book," and that, too, with a ring, which they borrowed. But another Sunday passed, before the formal application was made for due recognition of the church established by law in Great Britain. One would like to know where Mr. Ratcliffe went to meeting that day, or if he broke the strict Sabbath-keeping laws and stayed at home.

On Wednesday, however, May 26, "Mr. Ratcliffe, the minister, waits on the Council; Mr. Mason and Randolph propose that he may have one of the three Houses to preach in. That is deny'd, and he is granted the East-End of the Town House, where the Deputies used to meet, untill those who desire his Ministry shall provide a fitter place."

We can look around the Council board and see by the records who were present to consider this request, — Dudley, Stoughton, Fitz John and Wait Winthrop, Pynchon, Dudley, Wharton, Gedney, and E. Tyng. We may well regret that Sewall was not a councillor, and that no record is preserved of that scene, — the gloom and hesitation on the brow of the majority of the Council, determined to oppose as far as they can, yet afraid to oppose too far, and troubled by the thought that there is one among them who will report everything at home in England. If you will look at the portrait of William Stoughton, in the Memorial Hall of Harvard College, painted in his old age, you will perhaps think with me that the pinched and worried expression dates from this anxious moment. Mason and Randolph, however, are triumphant.

Dudley is full of perplexity. He knows well that if he favors one inch of concession he will lose his last hold on the people, who distrust him; that if he does not, he will offend Randolph, — and he dares not kick away that ladder of his fortune. He still wears the long straight Puritan hair and has the Puritan cast of face. The day will come when he will return from England to be Governor, with huge wig and the look of a man of the world; but he has not yet emerged from the chrysalis.

A good and honest bearing, and that of an English gentleman, is that of Rev. Robert Ratcliffe, — "a sober, prudent gent, and well approved," wearing the long black cassock of his calling; "a very Excellent Preacher, whose Matter was good, and the Dress in which he put it Extraordinary, he being as well an Orator as a Preacher." In graceful, dignified speech he asks that the King's church may have a fit shelter in the King's most loyal colony, and then withdraws, while the debate is urged with hot and bitter words.

And now turn from the debate on this all-engrossing subject, which must have thrilled from the town-house throughout the little town, and try to picture to yourselves the state of mind of the Puritans when they think how their one public building, the symbol and shelter of the highest authority of the Commonwealth, is given up to this use, — the Puritan State taking, as it were, under the wing of its sanction (though with an ill-grace) the representative of that which cast the fathers out from the mother-country! We are not left to imagination; for one of them has outlined his feelings in his diary. Turning to the left from the corner of Prison Lane, passing the Old Church as it looks grimly across the way at the new sight, leaving the porticoed town-house behind you, while a company of men and boys watches curiously to see if Mr. Ratcliffe will come in his surplice, or, like the ministers of the town, in Geneva gown and bands, — walk with me up "the Broad Street" (which took its later name from Washington's triumphal passage over it more than a century later), as it leads past the Third Meeting-house toward Roxbury. And now here is Captain Samuel Sewall's house[1] on "Seven Star Lane" (which we know as Summer Street), the home which his wife had inherited from her father John Hull, the famous mint-master. On this mild May morning the window is left ajar, and we can hear the family prayers. An eight year old boy is reading. "My Son reads to me in course the 26th of Isaiah, — 'In that day shall this Song be sung,' etc. And we sing the 141st Psalm, both exceedingly suited to this day, wherein there is to be worship according to the Church of England, as 't is called, in the Town-House, by Countenance of Authority." The psalm rises on the still air, in the rugged version of the Bay Psalm Book, to one of the old tunes which Sewall delighted to sing. "Set a watch, O Lord, before my mouth; keep the door of my lips. ... Incline not my heart ... to practise wicked works with men that work iniquity, and let me not eat of their dainties. When their judges are over-

[1] The letter from Dr. Estes Howe to Mr. Charles Deane, printed in the Proceedings of the Massachusetts Historical Society (second series, i. 312-326), demonstrates that Sewall resided here, and not in the house also owned by him, with casement of diamond panes set in lead, built by Sir Henry Vane, and where John Cotton once dwelt, "at a distance from other buildings and in winter very bleake," on the eastern slope of Beacon Hill, near our Pemberton Square of to-day.

thrown in stony places, they shall hear my words. Let the wicked fall into their own nets, whilst that I escape." And then the father of the family prays, doubtless in a tone and strain whose keynote was sounded by the Scripture lesson.

So was it, probably, in hundreds of old-fashioned Boston homes, as well as Sewall's, on that day when "worship according to the Church of England" was "in the Town House, by Countenance of Authority."

Yet there were other Christian homes, religious and devout, which retained a fresher and more loving memory of the hallowed usages of the mother-country, where those who had not breathed the New England air long enough to be weaned from Old England, and who did not share in the reverence for the usages of strict Puritanism or sympathize with much of its spirit, felt at last the loosening of bonds which had fretted them. To them those other words of the Scripture, which I have taken as my text, might well have seemed a gracious prophecy, as they saw a shoot from the stately Church of England set in the very high places of the Puritan Zion: "Thus saith the Lord God; I will also take of the highest branch of the high cedar, and will set it; I will crop off from the top his young twigs a tender one, and will plant it upon a high mountain and eminent; In the mountain of the height of Israel will I plant it: it shall bring forth boughs, and bear fruit, and be a goodly cedar."

Before us to-day there wait in this communion service the sacred emblems of that life which was lived and died for all men, and which in passing into human history transfigured that history forever. Our thoughts of controversy and strife may have seemed to draw us far away from those which gather closest around the Lord's Table. Yet not wholly so; for the very earnestness of the dispute showed that the hearts and souls of men were deeply engaged; and every thought of faithfulness and of duty leads us straight to him from whom his followers learn how conscience may inspire self-sacrifice, and how greater than whole burnt-offerings is a loving spirit.

been left to us by the fathers, we should all agree that neither gothic roofs nor fronts of carven stone ennobled it above its proper worth as the centre, not merely of a town history, but of the formation and crystallizing period of a great people; and our Roland would typify not merely the commercial freedom of a city, but the imperial freedom of a nation.

And yet, to the discerning eye, that primitive town-house had in its very homeliness and simplicity a truer fitness to the people who had built it, and whose convenience it served, than the stateliest edifice of Old World fame. As you stand at Salem in the little building of the First Church, — whose rude framework, rescued a few years ago from the barn in whose disguise it had been securely hidden for nearly two centuries, — and seem to hear those rough timbers, just squared with the broadaxe, echo the tones of Hugh Peter and Roger Williams, you feel that you are veritably in one of the *incunabula gentium*, — a place where a nation was cradled.

So might you feel, in a measure also, if you were to be landing with Rev. Robert Ratcliffe at this town of less than two thousand houses and eight thousand people, a third of them men trained to arms. The three hills, severally capped by a beacon, a windmill, and a fort; the houses clustered beneath them, close together along the shore, and farther back scattered among gardens; the busy "fairs," such as Josselyn saw them; and "on the south a small but pleasant common, where the gallants, a little before sunset, walk with their marmalet-madams till the nine o'clock bell rings them home to their respective habitations," — are a pleasant picture after a long voyage. "The buildings of Boston," said an impudent visitor, "like the women, are neat and handsome; their streets, like the hearts of the male inhabitants, paved with pebbles." Up such a rough-shod way, the broad main street, you hobble, and soon come to the town-house, built with Captain Robert Keayne's legacy, "upon pillars, where the merchants may confer," a space only partially enclosed, while "in the chambers above they keep their monthly courts." With belfry and sun-dial and balcony and outside staircase, and stocks and pillory under its shadow, this is evidently the centre and heart of the town. A few steps away stands the mother church; and two main arteries stretch off, one to the northern ferry over the Charles, the other to the south, "where the public gibbet creaked horribly in the wind, and the peninsula contracted to a narrow isthmus, over which passed the single great road from the metropolis. Tributary lanes, like rivulets, everywhere followed the natural conformation of the ground."

I spoke before of the opening act of the exciting drama, when Rev. Robert Ratcliffe stood before the council and obtained his petition for a place of worship, they granting him the use of the library in the town-house till they who desire his ministrations shall provide a fitter place.

It was, however, another week before the worship was really held, as "a movable pulpit" had to be provided, "carried up and down stairs, as occasion serves." "It seems," says Sewall, "many crowded thither." On the 15th of June, 1686, a meeting for organization was held "by the members of the Church of England, as by law established under the gracious influence of the most illustrious Prince, our Sovereign Lord James the II., by the Grace of God, of England, Scotland, France, and Ireland king, defendour of the faith, etc., . . . at Boston, within his said Majestie's territory and dominion of New England in America." It was here voted to send "an humble address" to the King "to implore his Majestie's favour to our church," and to write to the Archbishop of Canterbury and the Bishop of London. Also "Agreed, that Mr. Smith the joyner do make 12 formes for the service of the church, for each of which he shall be paid 4s. 8d. Agreed, with the said Mr. Smith the joyner, that this church will pay and allow unto him 20s. 18d. quarterlie, and every quarter, for and in consideration of his cleaning, placing, and removing the pulpit, forms, table, etc., and doing all other things which shall be convenient and necessary in our place of publique Assembling."

This was "to furnish the library room in the Town House in a decent manner, for the performance of divine service. . . . This was truly an humble beginning for those who made such high pretensions as did these zealous royalists and churchmen. As they assembled in the east end of the town-house, and looked round on their twelve forms and their movable pulpit, they must have felt the contrast between such a tabernacle and the solemn old cathedrals at home; and have felt too that they were among a people who, though of the same blood with themselves, were strangers to their mode of faith and worship, despising what they esteemed most sacred, and setting at nought the power which they deemed unquestionable. It is hardly to be supposed that these feelings were calculated to conciliate them toward the Congregationalists, or that the condition in which they found themselves was favorable at the time to their growth in Christian humility or charity."

The wonderful thing was, certainly, that they should find themselves in the town-house at all; and it shows how far the spirit of the colony was under the dread of English power. But when it came to any concession beyond, even the Council or a majority of them, though it contained Dudley, Mason, and Randolph, was firm. A fortnight later, July 1, a paper from "Mr. Robert Ratcliffe, desiring an honorable maintainance and good encouragement suitable for a minister of the Church of England," was read at the council meeting, and in answer it was "ordered that the contribution money collected in the church where he performs divine service be solely applied to the maintainance of Mr. Ratcliffe." No extreme concession, certainly. So the minister was left to the £50 a year which was thus collected.

And now if we pass out of the council chamber, where doubtless this proposition has been hotly debated, and where Randolph had been greatly disgusted at the flinching of Dudley (whom he had put in power) from carrying out his will, into the library room, we can catch glimpses of the scene. Even the Puritan diarist, though he deemed its presence there a pollution, and "dehorted" his family from entering such assemblies, somehow knew what was going on. When "one Mr. Clark, preacher at the town-house, speaks much against the Presbyterians in England and here," he hears the echo; and when "one Robison, Esq., that came from Antego, is buried with the common prayer, and first was had to the town-house and set before the pulpit;" and when on "Sabbath day, August 8, 't is said the sacrament of the Lord's Supper is administered at the town-house," — he notes, "Cleverly there."

Meantime, Randolph was writing home, with touches that add vividness to the picture: —

"Our company increasing beyond the expectation of the governt, we now use ye exchange, and have ye common prayer and two sermons every Sunday, and at 7 o'clock in ye morning on Wednesdays and Frydays the whole service of ye church. . . . To humour the people our minister preaches twice a day and baptises all that come to him, — some infants, some adult persons. We . . . resolve not to be baffled by the great affronts, — some calling our minister Baal's priest, and some of their ministers from the pulpit calling our praiers leeks, garlick, and trash. . . . To all my crimes [I have] added this one as the greatest in bringing the letherdge[1] and cerimonise of the Church of England to be observed amongst us."

But there were those who did not, like Randolph, write letters, whose feelings we must try to penetrate, if we would understand why the Church of England ought to have been allowed here, and how it won its way,— those to whom that little library room at the east end of the town-house was like the chamber looking toward the sun-rising, in which Bunyan's pilgrim lay till the dawn, and arose and sang a hymn. "In the most contentious and stormy periods," says Dr. Greenwood, "I doubt not that a holy calm was shed upon the heart of many a worshipper as he offered up his prayers in the way which to him was best and most affecting, and perhaps the way in which, long years ago, he had offered them up in some ivy-clad village church of green England, with many dear friends about him, now absent or dead. And when they celebrated their first communion, on the second Sabbath in August, 1686, I am fully persuaded that it was celebrated in that small room which they held by sufferance, and round that 'table' which was their cheap and lately constructed altar, with as much reverence and humility and edification as it was in any church or meeting-house in Old England or New."

The occupancy of the town-house was long enough to give the spot indelible associations, yet not so long as the Puritans may have desired. For

---

[1] The misspelling is probably due to the mistake of a copyist.

already in the same July came the report that Dudley's presidency would be only brief, and in December his rumored successor arrived. The extremists among the churchmen had doubtless been content to await his coming, in hopes of seeing more energetic measures adopted. They started a subscription paper, indeed, for money to build a church for themselves; but there seem not to have been enough of them to prosper greatly with this, from their own resources, and a sufficient motive was wanting to persuade the Puritan party to contribute. Sewall records that Randolph asked him to do so, but "seemed displeased because he spoke not up to it." The temporary occupation of the town-house continued, therefore, unchanged through that summer and autumn of 1686; and there Sir Edmund Andros found the little nursling of the English church feebly housed from the wintry climate of New England, when on the 20th of December he landed, the representative of the Roman Catholic king who was *ex officio* head of Church as well as of State.

The moment we speak of Andros, a wide and tempting field opens before us, which would lead us beyond our subject and quite outside the doors of the old town-house, although indeed it is around that building that the whole of that pictorial chapter of our colonial history seems to revolve, from the day of his triumphal entry into it to the memorable April day, twenty-eight months after, when the "declaration" deposing him was read from its gallery, and he was brought to it a prisoner. But our field of vision to-day only sees him as now the pivotal person in the questions which arose at once concerning the Church of England here.

We see him then on that December twentieth landing " at Governor Leverett's wharf about 2 P. M., where the president, etc., met him, and so march up through the Guards of the 8 Companyes to the Town House, where part of the Commission read." Whether the sentence was read we are not told, which enjoined " that such especially as shall be conformable to the rites of the Church of England be particularly countenanced and encouraged;" but his first act was to carry out its spirit. He takes the oath of allegiance, and as governor, then putting on his hat in token of superiority, administers the oaths to the councillors. Then entering the library room he "speaks to the ministers there about Accommodation as to a Meeting-house, that might so contrive the time as one House might serve two Assemblies." Perhaps the pinched and bare furnishings of the little room which he looked round upon stirred his choler (which lay near the surface of his mind), as he thought how these Congregationalists were housed in spacious temples. Perhaps the tempter, in the shape wherein the Puritan party almost believed him to be incarnated — in the person of Randolph — was at his ear with his favorite suggestion. Perhaps this point had been pressed upon him before embarking for America, by the Bishop of London. So arbitrary a measure does not, however, accord with the just and liberal character of Bishop Compton, who was, besides, secluded from the discharge of his great office at the time when Andros was preparing to sail from England, having been summoned for contempt by King James's Ecclesiastical Commission on August 3d and suspended on September 6, 1686, while the bishopric was administered by a commission headed by the notorious Sprat. But according to a letter of Randolph to Archbishop Sancroft, dated August 2, 1686, that dignitary had been "pleased to propose, when these matters were debated at the Councill Table," that "we should have . . . one of the churches in Boston." The idea is more in harmony with the high prerogative opinions of Sancroft. However this may be, there is to my mind no more striking grouping of vividly colored contrasts to be found in our early history than the scene which Sewall's Diary has preserved to us in scantiest outline, when in that moment in the library room of the old town-house the power of Great Britain, in the person of the King's governor, met the persistent resistance of New England Puritanism, in the person of the Boston ministers, face to face.

Andros stands with easy dignity and conscious power, not clad, as we see him in his portrait, in the shining breastplate which so well befits a soldier, but as a gentleman of the court, "in a scarlet coat laced," with lace falling from his sleeves, and in a rich cravat at his neck, the flowing hair or wig, as becomes a cavalier, increasing his resemblance to the Stuart sovereigns whom he served; an aquiline nose, a flashing eye, — the bearing of a man who had braved danger in soldierly campaigns; altogether a different figure from any that had been seen here. Able, imperious, an honest servant of the despot to whom he believed his loyalty was only due, let us give him his deserts of respect, though we do not love him, and are thankful that the cause which he stood for went down in wreck. Our history is infinitely richer because only one Andros was possible for us; and it is more picturesque because there was *one.*

Over against him is another group of five men in sombre clerical dress, their look and bearing always austere, and probably specially so at this moment. They have come with the other dignitaries to welcome him with fit respect, but with no intention of receiving his commands. He may bear himself like a courtier, but they are not the less ambassadors of the Highest; and some of them could stand in any assembly with Andros as peers in self-possession and in dignity, and one of them certainly is to prove himself more than his peer in statesmanship before this controversy is done. To Andros probably, at this moment, Increase Mather seemed a very insignificant personage; but he found his mistake later. When Boston has time to go back and gather up the remains of those who have deserved most, no memorial tablet or statue will be deemed too good for the man who procured us the charter of William and Mary. His face also is preserved to us, — the countenance of a Puritan scholar, thoughtful, refined, severe. The lineaments of Willard, also, of the South Church are perpetuated in a frontispiece to his "Body of Divinity,"—a typical Puritan face, lined with thought and care. And with them in the group are Cotton Mather, young and full of promise, with most of his books still lying unwritten in his busy, restless brain; and Allen of the First Church, rich and hospitable; and his colleague Joshua Moodey, who having been imprisoned in Portsmouth for his Puritan conscience by one governor, is not likely to be very compliant with the request of another,—as typical a group in our New England history as the famous five members of Parliament in that momentous scene which was like the stroke of destiny for Charles I.

Behind them is the whole passive resisting force of the substance of New England, when they give answer, after a day's interval for consultation, that they "cannot with a good conscience consent y^t our Meeting-House should be made use of for ye Common-pray^r worship." Nor can there be a doubt that when Sir Edmund finally determined, as the Passion Week of 1687 drew near, to take possession of the South Church for his own church service, he really did as much to prepare his downfall as when he acted on the theory that the title of Massachusetts land-owners from the Indians was "worth no more than the scratch of a bear's paw."

The reasonable desire of Englishmen belonging to the non-Puritan second emigration, here on English soil, for the worship and the ordinances of their own church, won its rights when backed by the strong secular arm of governors commissioned by the Crown to rule an English province as other English provinces were ruled, at that time, the world over. In the theories of both sides equally, Church and State were blended in seventeenth century fashion. Yet were they wholly wrong? Rather were they both sublimely true in their ground-thought, that the Commonwealth was divinely ordained. But the Puritan conception of Church and State was the seed-grain of future independence; while the new thought that was planted here two hundred years ago was the old thought so dear to the mother-country, of English law and English loyalty bound fast about the ancient throne of England by bonds of faith and prayer. Though the time came at last for separation, nevertheless was that English root one through which came great and enduring gifts to our country.

What followed this opening moment in our history will doubtless be described by others in its pictorial and dramatic setting. It is enough for us now to linger on this threshold of the narrative.

For the present, then, we see the Governor putting up with the "12 formes" and "the movable pulpit" in the town-house, where there was scant room for the increasing company of worshippers. Thither he goes, when January 25 "is kept for Saint Paul," and when, "Monday, January 31, there is a meeting at the Town House, forenoon and afternoon (Bell

rung for it), respecting the beheading Charles the
First. Governour there; very bad going by reason
of the watery snow." There, then, we leave him, as
we turn away from that scene of Old World loyalty
in this uncongenial clime, — around him the group
of courtiers from England or New York, and those
whom the New England bitterness regarded as rene-
gades, most of the gay apparel and of the fashion
that cast a gleam of brightness on the sombre hue
of Puritan Boston, officers in scarlet uniforms and
the Governor's guardsmen, and in the midst Rev.
Robert Ratcliffe reading those passages in which
the account of the passion of Christ is applied to
the blessed martyr, Charles I., while the congregation devoutly respond: "They shed the blood of
the just in the midst of Jerusalem;" "How is he
numbered with the children of God, and his lot is
among the saints." And if we listen for the faint
echoes of the preacher's words, we can hear them
in the rubric for the "Form of prayer with fasting,
to be used yearly on the 30th of January, being the
day of the martyrdom of the blessed King Charles
the First, to implore the mercy of God that neither
the guilt of that sacred and innocent blood, nor
those other sins by which God was provoked to deliver up both us and our king into the hands of
cruel and unreasonable men, may at any time here-
after be visited upon us or our posterity;" which en-
joins that "After the Nicene creed, shall be read,
instead of the sermon for that day, the first and
second parts of the homily against disobedience

and wilful rebellion, set forth by authority; or the minister who officiates shall preach a sermon of his own composing upon the same argument."

And the words of solemn prayer rise from the preacher's lips there in the town-house of New England's Puritan people: "We acknowledge it Thine especial favor, that, though for our many and great provocations Thou didst suffer Thine anointed, blessed King Charles the First (as on this day), to fall into the hands of violent and bloodthirsty men, and barbarously to be murdered by them, yet Thou didst not leave us forever as sheep without a shepherd, but by Thy gracious providence did miraculously preserve the undoubted heir of his crowns, our then gracious sovereign King Charles the Second, from his bloody enemies, hiding him under the shadow of Thy wings until their tyranny was overpast. . . . Grant to our gracious sovereign, King James, a long and happy reign over us." And Governor and people say, Amen.

In such forms as these, discarded now (and only within the memory of many of us) by the Church of England itself, we can see one reason why the forefathers of New England did not love or welcome the church which bore them as its fruit. Yet even in these there was a reaching out through the earthly loyalty after something which we may well desire even in our new age, and which we who have known the story that is written on the soldiers' monument by our western portal, ought to understand. I mean the spirit which honors and reveres that which is over it by the ordination of God, and can even suffer and die for it.

It was in the spirit of such old-fashioned loyalties that the church, which was soon built to relieve the South Meeting-house of its unwelcome tenants, took from the beginning, as a matter of course, the name of King's Chapel. And by a fine felicity, as an illustration how the loyalties which fitly belonged here while we were English subjects could be continued on a higher plane and in a loftier key after the royal province became the commonwealth in the great republic, the name was continued after the Revolution in token of loyalty to "the King of Kings."

So, then, was set here a shoot of the English vine; and we who owe to it the heritage of holy and reverend usages and prayers made dear by ancient devotion, and so much of Christian faith and spiritual help for which the church stands to us, may well be grateful and remember.

Not only the church which was thus first sheltered in the old town-house, but all that family of churches which are descended from the mother church of England, may well look upon that spot as the cradle of their faith. And more than that, the fact should be imperishably connected with that spot, that — though against the will of New England and by some constraint of royal power — the old town-house was the first spot where freedom of religious worship was recognized as "by authority," where the ancient order began to give place to the modern world.

Our festival, then, will be not merely the family gathering of an old historical parish. It commemorates the founding on New England soil of the church from which, under God's providence, has come a great branch of the Christian Church in America, in whose wide spread of Christian work, in all that it is doing to make the gospel a power of life to this great country, we may well say with the apostle: " I therein do rejoice; yea, and will rejoice."

The planting of this church was amid opposition and bitterness, and its history for the first century scarred as that of no other church that I know by the controversies, both political and theological, which marked that hundred years in our American history. It is not to dwell upon that side of the story that we shall hold our commemoration. Yet we remember it as one honorable and memorable, and not a little part of the great history of the land; and thankful that the shadows of old disputes and alienations in that remote past have so far died away, we reach forth to those on the one side or on the other, from whose fathers the forefathers of this church were parted in the earnestness of their loyalty and the strength of their conviction, the hand of fraternal good-will, of Christian love and mutual charity, praying that they and we may be builded up in the faith of our common Master, " both theirs and ours."

As Mr. Greenwood, half a century ago, spoke of our predecessors: " I must observe that if we have not more truth we certainly have more peace than they. This is to be attributed chiefly to the change of our political and ecclesiastical condition. . . . From the very time of our severance from the mother Church and the parent State there has been not a single disagreement . . . from any cause, so far as I can learn. The words of the prophet . . . sound like prophecy for us. 'The glory of this latter house shall be greater than that of the former, saith the Lord of hosts, and in their place will I give peace, saith the Lord of hosts.' So may it ever be. 'Peace be within thy walls! — for my brethren and companions' sakes, I will wish thee prosperity.'"

1686.   1886.

Commemorative Services

KING'S CHAPEL, BOSTON,

UPON THE

COMPLETION OF TWO HUNDRED YEARS.

WEDNESDAY, DECEMBER 15, 1886,

AT 2 P.M.

TOGETHER WITH SOME HISTORICAL MEMORIALS.

Committee of Arrangements.

WILLIAM PERKINS, *President.*	J. RANDOLPH COOLIDGE, Jr., *Secretary.*
J. TEMPLEMAN COOLIDGE, 3d.	
GREELY S. CURTIS.	A. LAWRENCE LOWELL.
EDWARD S. GREW.	FRANCIS C. LOWELL.
THOMAS B. HALL.	THOMAS MINNS.
GEORGE HIGGINSON.	GEORGE R. MINOT.
PATRICK T. JACKSON.	CHARLES E. SAMPSON.
HORACE A. LAMB.	ROGER WOLCOTT.

Rev. HENRY W. FOOTE, *Minister.*

Boston in New-England
Anno Domini 1686.

An entry booke of all such meetings, Agreements and other matters, proper to be Recognized, had, and done from time to time, by the members of the Church of England, as by Law established, under the Gracious influences of ye most illustrious Prince our Sovraign Lord, James the 2d By the Grace of God, of England, Scotland, France, and Ireland King, defendour of ye faith &c. Anno Domini 1686 and in ye 2d Yeare of said Majesties Reign, at Boston within his said majesties Territorys and Dominion of New-England In America.

FIRST PAGE OF THE EARLIEST RECORD BOOK.

ORDER OF SERVICES.

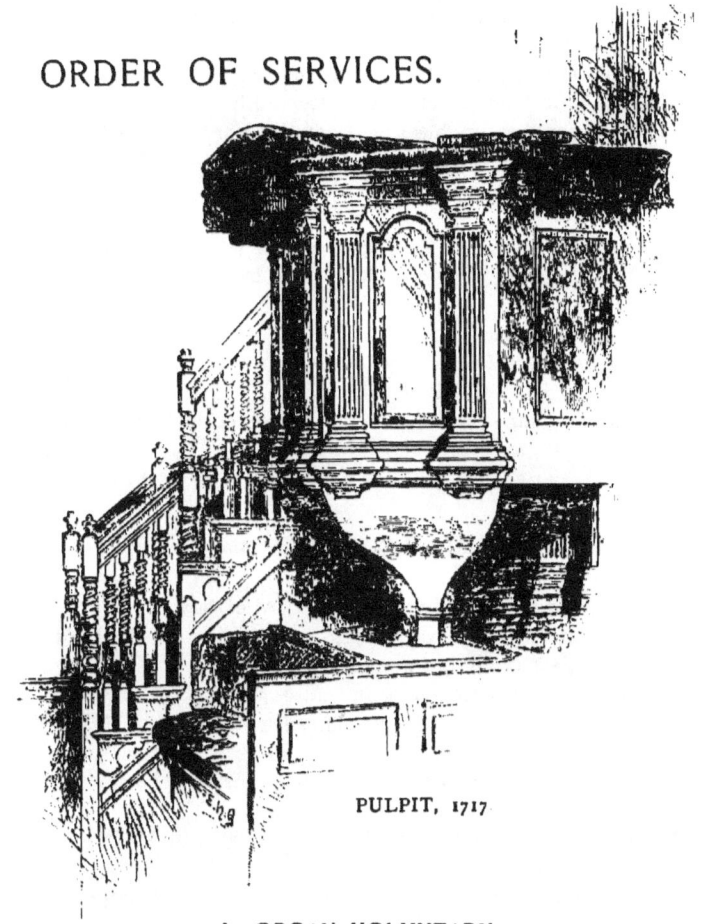

PULPIT, 1717

I. ORGAN VOLUNTARY.

II. ADDRESS OF WELCOME.
WILLIAM MINOT, Esq.

III. PSALMS.
(*To be read responsively.*)

PSALM XXIV. — *Domini est terra.*

THE earth is the Lord's, and the fulness thereof; the world, and they that dwell therein.

For he hath founded it upon the seas, and established it upon the floods.

Who shall ascend into the hill of the Lord? or who shall stand in his holy place?

He that hath clean hands, and a pure heart; who hath not lifted up his soul unto vanity, nor sworn deceitfully.

He shall receive the blessing from the Lord, and righteousness from the God of his salvation

This is the generation of them that seek him, that seek thy face, O Jacob.

Lift up your heads, O ye gates; and be ye lift up, ye everlasting doors; and the King of glory shall come in.

Who is this King of glory? The Lord strong and mighty, the Lord mighty in battle.

Lift up your heads, O ye gates; even lift them up, ye everlasting doors; and the King of glory shall come in.

Who is this King of glory? The Lord of hosts, he is the King of glory. *Amen.*

PSALM LXXXIV. — *Quam dilecta.*

How amiable are thy tabernacles, O Lord of hosts!

My soul longeth, yea, even fainteth for the courts of the Lord; my heart and my flesh crieth out for the living God.

Yea, the sparrow hath found an house, and the swallow a nest for herself, where she may lay her young, even thine altars, O Lord of hosts, my King and my God.

Blessed are they that dwell in thy house: they will be still praising thee.

Blessed is the man whose strength is in thee; in whose heart are the ways of them.

Who passing through the valley of Baca make it a well; the rain also filleth the pools.

They go from strength to strength, every one of them in Zion appeareth before God.

O Lord God of hosts, hear my prayer; give ear, O God of Jacob.

Behold, O God our shield, and look upon the face of thine anointed.

For a day in thy courts is better than a thousand. I had rather be a doorkeeper in the house of my God, than to dwell in the tents of wickedness.

For the Lord God is a sun and shield: the Lord will give grace and glory; no good thing will he withhold from them that walk uprightly.

O Lord of hosts, blessed is the man that trusteth in thee.

Amen.

PSALM CXXII.—*Lætatus sum.*

I was glad when they said unto me, Let us go into the house of the Lord.
Our feet shall stand within thy gates, O Jerusalem.
Jerusalem is builded as a city that is compact together;
Whither the tribes go up, the tribes of the Lord, unto the testimony of Israel, to give thanks unto the name of the Lord.
For there are set thrones of judgment, the thrones of the house of David.
Pray for the peace of Jerusalem: they shall prosper that love thee
Peace be within thy walls, and prosperity within thy palaces.
For my brethren and companions' sakes, I will now say, Peace be within thee.
Because of the house of the Lord our God I will seek thy good.

Amen.

IV. SCRIPTURE LESSON.

V. COLLECTS.

VI. PRAYER.

The Rev. FREDERICK AUGUSTUS FARLEY, D.D., of Brooklyn, N.Y.

VII. PSALM LXXXIV.

"*WINCHESTER TUNE.*"

From Playford's "Whole Book of Psalms,"
1613-1693.—*Various Editions.*

PSALM LXXXIV.

1. How pleasant is thy dwelling place,
   O Lord, of hosts, to me!
   The tabernacles of thy grace,
   how pleasant, Lord, they be!

2. My soul doth long full sore to go
   into thy courts abroad:
   My heart and flesh cry out also
   for thee the living God.

3. For why? within thy courts one day
   is better to abide,
   Than other-where to keep or stay
   a thousand days beside.

4. Much rather had I keep a door
   within the house of God,
   Than in the tents of wickedness
   to settle my abode.

5. For God the Lord, light and defence
    will grace and glory give;
And no good thing will he with-hold
    from them that purely live.

6. O Lord of hosts, that man is blest,
    and happy sure is he,
That is persuaded in his breast
    to trust all times in thee.

VIII. ADDRESSES.

The Rev. HENRY WILDER FOOTE, the Minister.

His Excellency the Governor of Massachusetts,
GEORGE DEXTER ROBINSON, LL.D.

IX. HYMN.

WILLIAM EVERETT, PH. D.

To be sung by the Congregation to the tune of ST. THOMAS. *(By request.)*

COME to thy house, O King!
    To thee thy people kneel;
Accept the homage that they bring,
    And all thy grace reveal.

For ten score years this ground
    Service and song hath known,
From hearts that sought thee in the sound
    Of worship all their own.

The ancient and the new,
    The ordered and the free,
The elders' trust, the prophets' view,
    Blend in our rites to thee.

And still let age to age,
    Through triumph and through loss,
Walk by that pure and hallowed page,
    Dear Saviour, to thy cross.

Bind by thy gospel's tie
    The future to the past,
And, as the fathers' earliest cry,
    Hear thou the children's last.

X. ADDRESSES.

The Rev. GEORGE EDWARD ELLIS, D.D., LL.D.,
President of the Massachusetts Historical Society.

The Rev. GEORGE ANGIER GORDON, Minister of the Old South Church.

XI. PSALM XXIII.

"*YORK TUNE.*"

Taken from "A very plain and easy Introduction to the Art of Singing Psalm Tunes. By Rev. JOHN TUFTS, of the Second Church. Newbury, 1712."

From Mather's "Psalterium Americanum."

THE BOOK OF PSALMS, in a Translation Exactly conformed unto the Original, but all in Blank Verse, fitted unto the Tunes commonly used in our Churches. Boston: in N. E. 1718.

---

1. My Shepherd is th' ETERNAL God; ‖ I shall not be in (Any) want: ‖

2. In pastures of a tender grass ‖ He (Ever) makes me to lie down: ‖ To waters of tranquillities ‖ He gently carries me, (Along.) ‖

3. My *feeble and my wandering* Soul ‖ He (Kindly) does fetch back again; ‖ In the plain paths of righteousness ‖ He does lead (And guide) me along, ‖ because of the regard He has ‖ (Ever) unto His *Glorious* Name. ‖

4. Yea, when I shall walk in the Vale ‖ of the dark (dismal) shade of Death, ‖ I'll of no evil be afraid, ‖ because thou (ever) art with me. ‖ Thy rod and thy staff, these are what ‖ yield (constant) comfort unto me.

5. A table thou dost furnish out ‖ richly (for me) before my face. ‖ 'T is in view of mine Enemies; ‖ (And then) my head thou dost anoint ‖ with fatning and perfuming Oil: ‖ my cup it (ever) overflows. ‖

6. Most certainly the thing that is ‖ Good, with (most kind) Benignity, ‖ *This* all the days that I do live ‖ shall (still and) ever follow me; ‖ Yea, I shall dwell, and Sabbatize, ‖ even to (unknown) length of days, ‖ *Lodg'd* in the House which does belong ‖ to (Him who's) the ETERNAL God. ‖

XII. ADDRESSES.

CHARLES WILLIAM ELIOT, LL.D., President of Harvard University.
The Rev. PHILLIPS BROOKS, D.D., Rector of Trinity Church.

XIII. MAGNIFICAT IN F.
(B. TOURS.)

XIV. ADDRESS.
The Rev. JOHN HOPKINS MORISON, D.D.

XV. HYMN.
OLIVER WENDELL HOLMES, M.D., LL.D., D.C.L.

(To be sung by the Congregation to the tune of TALLIS'S EVENING HYMN.)

O'ERSHADOWED by the walls that climb,
    Piled up in air by living hands,
A rock amid the waves of time,
    Our grey old house of worship stands.

High o'er the pillared aisles we love
    The symbols of the past look down;
Unharmed, unharming, throned above,
    Behold the mitre and the crown!

Let not our younger faith forget
    The loyal souls that held them dear;
The prayers we read their tears have wet,
    The hymns we sing they loved to hear.

The memory of their earthly throne
    Still to our holy temple clings,
But here the kneeling suppliants own
    One only Lord, the King of kings.

Hark! while our hymn of grateful praise
    The solemn echoing vaults prolong,
The far-off voice of earlier days
    Blends with our own in hallowed song:

To Him who ever lives and reigns,
    Whom all the hosts of Heaven adore,
Who lent the life His breath sustains,
    Be glory now and evermore!

XVI. ADDRESS.

The Rev. JAMES FREEMAN CLARKE, D.D.,
Minister of the Church of the Disciples.

XVII. POEM.

OLIVER WENDELL HOLMES, M.D., LL.D., D.C.L.

XVIII. ANTHEM.

(HÄNDEL, 1685-1759.)

Their bodies are buried in peace, but their name liveth evermore.

XIX. ADDRESSES.

The Rev. ANDREW PRESTON PEABODY, D.D., LL.D.,
Plummer Professor Emeritus in Harvard University.

The Rev. FRANCIS GREENWOOD PEABODY,
Plummer Professor in Harvard University.

XX. ANTHEM.

(ARTHUR S. SULLIVAN.)

Who is like unto thee, O Lord? Who is like thee, glorious in holiness, fearful in praises, doing wonders?

Thou in thy mercy hast led forth the people which thou hast redeemed.

Thou shalt bring them in, and plant them in the mountain of thine inheritance, in the place, O Lord, which thou hast made for thee to dwell in, in the Sanctuary, O Lord, which thy hands have established.

The Lord shall reign for ever and ever.

Sing ye to the Lord! Hallelujah! Amen.

XXI. BENEDICTION.

The Rev. JOHN CORDNER, LL.D.

PORTRAITS, FLAGS, AND ARMS.

The portraits of Royal Governors and others connected with King's Chapel have been kindly loaned by the Commonwealth; the Massachusetts Historical Society; the Misses Loring; and Mrs. George R. Minot.

The flags employed in the decoration of the interior are the British flags of 1686–1776; the flag of New England under Governor Andros; the flag of the Province of Massachusetts Bay previous to 1700; the Pine-Tree flag carried at the Siege of Louisburg; Patriot flags and flags of the Revolution, ending with the first American flag. The exterior decoration is a combination of several of these flags.

The Coats of Arms represented on the escutcheons are copies of those of persons belonging to the Parish of King's Chapel in the pre-Revolutionary period, most of them having at that time been placed in the church. They are those of —

1. His Honor Sir Francis Nicholson, Knt., Lieutenant-Governor.
2. His Excellency Joseph Dudley, Governor and Commander-in-Chief.
3. His Excellency Sir Edmund Andros, Knt., Governor and Commander-in-Chief.
4. His Excellency William Burnet, Governor and Commander-in-Chief.
5. The Foxcroft Family.
6. His Excellency Jonathan Belcher, Governor and Commander-in-Chief.
7. The Mountfort Family.
8. His Excellency the Earl of Bellomont, Governor and Commander-in-Chief.
9. His Excellency William Shirley, Governor and Commander-in-Chief.
10. His Excellency Thomas Pownall, Governor and Commander-in-Chief.
11. The Checkley Family.
12. His Excellency Colonel Samuel Shute, Governor and Commander-in-Chief.
13. The Rev. Roger Price, Rector of King's Chapel and Commissary of the Lord Bishop of London.
14. Capt. Francis Hamilton of His Majesty's Ship of War Kingfisher.

The Royal Escutcheon hung upon the front of the pulpit is the same which, until the Revolution, was placed over the door of the Province House, and is the property of the Massachusetts Historical Society.

PLACES OF WORSHIP.

THE first administration of the Prayers and Ordinances of the Church of England was in the old Town House, May 30, 1686. The first meeting for organization was on June 15, and the first administration of the Lord's Supper was on August 2, 1686. Occupancy of the South Meeting-House, March 25, 1687 to 1689. First King's Chapel, built of wood, and opened for service June 30, 1689, was known as "Queen's Chapel" during the reign of Queen Anne. Present church erected 1754.

The first royal Governor connected with the church was SIR EDMUND ANDROS, Knt. Eight of his successors have worshipped here, occupying the Governor's pew as representatives of the Crown,— JOSEPH DUDLEY, SAMUEL SHUTE, WILLIAM BURNET, JONATHAN BELCHER, WILLIAM SHIRLEY, THOMAS POWNALL, SIR FRANCIS BERNARD, Bart., and GENERAL GAGE. The first service after the evacuation of Boston by the British troops in 1776 was the funeral of General Joseph Warren, whose body was brought from Bunker Hill. The congregation worshipped with Trinity Church during the Revolutionary War, permitting the Old South Church and Society to use King's Chapel from 1777 to 1782. The liturgy was altered from that of the Church of England in 1785.

ROLL OF MINISTERS AND KING'S LECTURERS OF KING'S CHAPEL.

NAME.	INDUCTED.	DIED OR REMOVED.
ROBERT RATCLIFFE, *Rector*	1686	1689
JOSIAH CLARKE, *Assistant*	1686	
SAMUEL MYLES, *Rector*	1689	1728
GEORGE HATTON, *Assistant*	1693	1696
CHRISTOPHER BRIDGE, *Queen's Lecturer*	1699	1706
HENRY HARRIS, *King's Lecturer*	1709	1729
ROGER PRICE, *Rector and Bishop's Commissary*	1729	1746
THOMAS HARWARD, *King's Lecturer*	1731	1736
ADDINGTON DAVENPORT, *King's Lecturer*	1737	1740
STEPHEN ROE, *Assistant*	1741	1744
HENRY CANER, D.D., *Rector*	1747	1776
CHARLES BROCKWELL, *King's Lecturer*	1747	1755
JOHN TROUTBECK, *King's Lecturer*	1755	1775
JAMES FREEMAN, *Reader*	1782	
JAMES FREEMAN, D.D., *Rector and Minister*	1787	1836
SAMUEL CARY, *Associate Minister*	1809	1815
FRANCIS WILLIAM PITT GREENWOOD, *Associate Minister*	1824	
FRANCIS WILLIAM PITT GREENWOOD, D. D., *Rector and Minister*	1836	1843
EPHRAIM PEABODY, D.D., *Minister*	1845	1856
HENRY WILDER FOOTE, *Minister*	1861	

First Church Wardens.

BENJAMIN BULLIVANT.   RICHARD BANKES.

WARDENS AND VESTRY. 1886–1887.

ARTHUR T. LYMAN, } *Wardens.*
CHARLES P. CURTIS, }
A. LAWRENCE LOWELL, *Treasurer.*
WILLIAM PERKINS.
PHILIP H. SEARS.
JOHN REVERE.*
GEORGE HIGGINSON.
PATRICK T. JACKSON.

GEORGE C. RICHARDSON.*
JOHN W. WHEELWRIGHT.
GREELY S. CURTIS.
THOMAS B. HALL.
ROBERT H. STEVENSON.
J. RANDOLPH COOLIDGE, JR.
ROGER WOLCOTT.

* Died 1886.

THE COMMUNION PLATE.

THE ancient Communion Plate of King's Chapel was the gift of the following Kings: WILLIAM and MARY, GEORGE II., GEORGE III. A portion of it was given by the Church before the Revolution to other parishes of the Church of England, on receiving later royal gifts. But that which was carried away by the last royalist rector on the evacuation of Boston by the British troops in March, 1776, amounted to twenty-eight hundred ounces of silver. The present Plate is the gift of members of the Church at different times, subsequently. Among the pieces are the following: —

1. A FLAGON. "King's Chapel, 1798."

2. A CHRISTENING BASIN. "King's Chapel, The Gift of EBENEZER OLIVER, Esq'., 1798."

3. A SALVER. "King's Chapel, 1798. This plate was given me at my birth by my Grand Father, NATH'. CARY, Esq'."

4. TWO OFFERTORY PLATES. "To King's Chapel, Easter, 1829. From JOSEPH MAY, of Boston."

5. TWO PATENS. "To King's Chapel, 1798. From Madam BULFINCH."

6. TWO CUPS. "To King's Chapel, Boston. From Mrs. CATHARINE COOLIDGE."

7. PLATE. "Presented to King's Chapel by JOHN L. GARDNER, 1868."

8. A SILVER CROSS, very richly wrought, from JAMES W. PAIGE.

9. A large and richly wrought CUP AND SALVER, the gift of many friends to the Rev. JAMES WALKER, D.D., LL.D., on his eightieth birthday, bequeathed by him to the Rev. SAMUEL OSGOOD, D.D., LL.D., of New York, in 1874, and by him presented to King's Chapel for communion use.

10. The handsome Communion Service which formerly belonged to the New North Church in Boston (founded in 1714). This service consists of TEN TANKARDS and CUPS, TWO FLAGONS, and ONE CHRISTENING BASIN, and was "Given to King's Chapel, Boston, by a few members of the Congregation, Easter, 1872," having been purchased by them on its sale in consequence of the dissolution of that ancient society. These pieces bear the coats-of-arms of the original donors and other inscriptions. Among the oldest is a Tankard, inscribed, "Given by Deacon JOHN BURNETT to ye New North Church 1714."

CHOIR.

ORGANIST AND MUSICAL DIRECTOR: JOHN W. TUFTS.

Sopranos.

Miss GERTRUDE FRANKLIN.*
Miss LOUISE ELLIOTT.
Miss ELENE BUFFINGTON KEHEW.

Altos.

Mrs. E. C. FENDERSON.*
Miss GERTRUDE EDMANDS.
Miss HARRIET A. WHITING.

Tenors.

Mr. J. C. BARTLETT.*
Mr. GEORGE J. PARKER.
Mr. GEORGE W. WANT.

Basses.

Dr. C. W. GODDARD.*
Mr. J. K. BERRY.
Mr. H. T. REMICK.

* Of the regular Choir.

USHERS.

FRANCIS BULLARD.
JOHN G. COOLIDGE.
CHARLES P. CURTIS, Jr.
WILLIAM ENDICOTT, 3D.
Dr. JOHN HOMANS, 2D.
ARTHUR LYMAN.
HERBERT LYMAN.

EDWARD B. ROBINS.
RICHARD SEARS.
LEMUEL STANWOOD.
CHARLES D. TURNBULL.
ARTHUR W. WHEELWRIGHT.
ELLERTON P. WHITNEY.
W. POWER WILSON.

COMMEMORATIVE SERVICES

BY

KING'S CHAPEL, BOSTON,

Upon the Completion of Two Hundred Years,

WEDNESDAY, DEC. 15, 1886.

COMMEMORATIVE SERVICES.

THE decoration of King's Chapel, both exterior and interior, for the occasion, was designed with the purpose of making everything employed illustrative of the unique and historic significance of the church. On the outside of the Chapel, over the front porch on the face of the tower behind the colonnade, was a tablet (six feet six inches by three feet six inches) surrounded by six colonial and patriot flags, extended over the main door and upon the walls on either side, — a total width of eighteen feet. A large palm-leaf, painted a dead green, extended across the tablet, upon which in a ribbon was written " King's Chapel, 1686–1886."

The flags, beginning at the left hand, were: First, the sea-colors of New England in use as early as the end of the seventeenth century; the British Union of 1707; the Pine-Tree flag of New England; the Grand-Union flag, first raised by Washington at the camp at Cambridge on Jan. 1, 1776; another early flag of New England; and the flag of New England sent by King James the Second with Governor Andros in 1686.

The interior decorations consisted of portraits of Royal Governors and others; of twenty-four Colonial and Revolutionary flags; of the coats-of-arms of the Governors and of other distinguished persons. The Governor's pew was restored, its dimensions remaining clearly outlined on the plaster ceiling, and its shape given by a drawing from memory by Miss Sarah H. Clarke.

The galleries of the Chapel are supported by eight Corinthian columns in pairs, which continue to the ceiling. On the bases of these columns were placed the portraits of several of the Royal Governors and of some noted persons who worshipped at King's Chapel, in the following order: —

> REBECCA, wife of Governor JOSEPH DUDLEY.
> Governor JOSEPH DUDLEY.
> Governor BURNET.
> Governor BELCHER, painted by F. Liopoldt in 1729, in London.
> Lieutenant-Governor DUMMER, said by tradition to have been painted by Lely or Kneller.
> Governor HUTCHINSON, painted by Edward Truman in 1741.
> Governor POWNALL, a copy, painted by Pratt, of the original portrait.
> PETER FANEUIL, painted by Smybert.
> Rev. JAMES FREEMAN, pastor of King's Chapel 1787–1836, painted by Guliger.

These portraits were kindly loaned by the Massachusetts Historical Society, with the exception of that of Governor Burnet, which hangs in the senate-chamber at the State

CAPT. HAMILTON'S
ARMS.*

ARMS OF BURNET.*

DAVENPORT ARMS.

ARMS OF SIR FRANCIS NICHOLSON, 1693.

DUDLEY ARMS.*

ARMS OF SHUTE.*

ARMS OF ANDROS.*

* The escutcheons marked with an asterisk are known to have hung in the first wooden King's Chapel.

ARMS OF BELCHER.*

PRICE COAT-OF-ARMS.

FOXCROFT ARMS.*

CHECKLEY ARMS.

ARMS OF SHIRLEY.

ARMS OF BELLOMONT.*

House; that of Lieutenant-Governor Dummer, belonging to the Misses Loring; and that of the Rev. James Freeman, belonging to the family of the late Mr. George Richards Minot. It was found to be impossible to obtain portraits of some persons pre-eminently associated with our history, — as Governors Andros and Shirley, — while some of those represented were only placed here officially, and not as worshipping here; but it was felt that they might properly be admitted as types of the period to which they belonged.

Upon the columns, directly over the portraits, were hung the escutcheons containing the coats-of-arms of the Governors and of other persons connected with the Chapel previous to the Revolution. The originals of most of these coats-of-arms were hung in the first, wooden Chapel. Beginning on the left hand with the arms of his Honor Sir FRANCIS NICHOLSON, Knight, Lieutenant-Governor, as in the list on the programme, the series ended on the right hand with those of Captain FRANCIS HAMILTON, of His Majesty's ship-of-war " Kingfisher," in 1687.

The front of the galleries is ornamented with raised panels, three between each set of columns, — twenty-four in all. Each of these panels contained a Colonial or a Revolutionary flag, beginning with the Cross of St. George, and ending with the first American flag unfurled at the battle of Brandywine, September, 1777. Among them was the flag of New England under Andros; the flag of the Province of Massachusetts Bay previous to 1700; the blue flag with the crescent raised on Fort Sullivan by Moultrie in 1775; the Pine-Tree flag of New England; the yellow field, with the coiled rattlesnake, — a flag often carried by the Patriots, and a favorite ornament on their drum-heads; the rattlesnake flag, with the motto " Don't tread on me," used by Paul Jones; a pine-tree flag, with rattlesnake coiled at its roots, — the flag hoisted by the Massachusetts State cruisers; the Beaver flag, used by the merchants of

New York before the Revolution; the Grand-Union flag of 1776; and a Revolutionary flag of Rhode Island.

The portraits, escutcheons, and flags were connected by a double garland of laurel.

The reading-desk was enveloped in a British flag; and the front of the organ loft was draped with large banners, representing the Lion of St. Andrew on a yellow ground, the pre-Revolutionary flags of New England, and the British Union Jack.

On the restored Governor's pew was placed the ancient crown from the top of the organ. In front of the pulpit hung the carved tablet bearing the Royal Arms of England which formerly hung over the door of the old Province House, and is now in the possession of the Massachusetts Historical Society. On the communion-table, beneath the windows of Munich glass which the late Mr. John Amory Lowell gave to the church, was spread the church silver, — embracing various pieces given by members of the parish in the last century, the beautiful memorial pieces of President James Walker, and the rich communion service formerly belonging to the New North Church, which was, on the dissolution of that ancient parish in 1873, bought and presented to King's Chapel by members of our congregation.

The Committee feel that the parish owe a special obligation to Mr. J. Templeman Coolidge, 3d, for the thorough care and artistic perfection with which the whole plan of decoration was arranged by him, and carried out in every detail, under his personal supervision, by Messrs. Savory and Son and Messrs. Lamprell and Marble.

The Committee were also much indebted to Mr. Robert S. Peabody, a son of the former minister of the church, for supervising the reconstruction of the old Governor's pew as it existed down to the year 1824.

Wednesday, December 15, had been selected for these services, as being the day of the month, though not the month itself, on which the exact anniversary of the first organization of the King's Chapel fell, the first meeting having been held June 15, the second July 4, and the first communion service on the second Sabbath in August. It being impossible in the summer season to gather together all whom it was desirable to have take part in our celebration, it was thought best to appoint the recollection of all these days at this later date. The weather was most propitious, — a clear, moderate, bright December day, though preceded and followed by days of storm. Eleven hundred and fifty tickets had been issued, and the church was thronged in every part. The arrangements for seating the audience were under the care of Mr. Roger Wolcott, assisted by twelve young men of the parish. The chancel was filled with seats for the occasion, which were occupied by the clerical speakers, and by many other prominent clergymen of the city, of different denominations. The Governor's pew as restored was occupied by his Excellency the Governor of the Commonwealth, his Honor the Lieutenant-Governor, his Honor the Mayor of the City of Boston, President Eliot of Harvard University, and Dr. Oliver Wendell Holmes, — the speakers being conducted from that pew to the reading-desk to make their addresses. The services began at two of the clock, and were intently listened to by the large audience to their close at twenty minutes before six.

The gentlemen invited to make addresses were selected as representing various historical associations of the church, or as being themselves in different ways connected with it. A descendant in the sixth generation of one of the original subscribers to build the first wooden church in 1689 presided. The religious services were conducted by the minister, together with the son of the revered Dr. Ephraim Peabody, and the grandson and namesake of one of the most honored wardens of the church in a former generation, Col. Joseph May. The Rev. Frederick A. Farley, D.D., of Brooklyn, N. Y., and the Rev. Thatcher Thayer, D.D., of Newport, R. I., who were both baptized by Dr. Freeman, and are among the oldest living descendants of the church, had also been invited to take part in the services, but were unable to be present. The Governor of the Commonwealth fitly spoke as the successor of eight of his pre-Revolutionary predecessors, and of Governor Gore, who all worshipped here. The President of the Massachusetts Historical Society also represented the First Church, the mother of the religious life of Boston. The connection of the Old South Church and of the Protestant Episcopal Church with the first hundred years of our history gave a peculiar fitness to the addresses of the minister of the Old South Church and the rector of Trinity Church; and the remaining speakers had equally significant reason for taking part in the services, — Dr. Holmes and Dr. Andrew P. Peabody being members of the present parish, while not only the honored ministry but even the names of the ministers during the second century, Drs. Freeman, Greenwood, and Ephraim Peabody, were recalled by those who spoke. To these should be added the name of the Rev. Samuel Cary, colleague minister from 1808 to 1815, a fitting tribute to whose memory is given in the letter of the Rev. Dr. Farley.

The music was arranged to show the progression from the English church-music in use at the time of the foundation of King's Chapel, and that in use in the Puritan meeting-houses of New England at about the same period, to the rich anthems of modern church-music. With the two beautiful hymns kindly written for this occasion, in the singing of which the whole congregation joined, the music was exquisitely rendered by a choir of twelve voices. The whole was under the direction of Mr. John W. Tufts, the organist and musical director of the church, to whose care much of the success was due.

In the evening a reception was held for the parish at the house of Mrs. GEORGE BATY BLAKE, 37 Beacon Street, which was attended by many members of the parish and by some other friends.

Nearly six hundred letters were received by the Committee from invited guests and others, a portion of which will be found in the Correspondence.

The services opened with an Organ Voluntary, followed by the Address of Welcome.

ADDRESS.

BY WILLIAM MINOT, ESQ.

LADIES AND GENTLEMEN, — It is my pleasant office to welcome you, on behalf of the congregation of King's Chapel, to the memorial celebration of the two hundredth anniversary of the foundation of this church. We gather here to renew our memories of the wise and gifted men who for two centuries, through all social and political changes and vicissitudes, have instructed the faith and promoted the piety of the numerous generations of their parishioners.

We keep with affectionate interest the birthdays of those we love. How much more should we hallow the birth-year of our church, which for so many generations has dispensed the abiding hope, the steadfast faith, the unfailing charity of the Christian religion!

How manifold are the associations with the building! The King's Chapel! That name alone is a monument, and one of the most interesting of monuments. It spans the two centuries which mark the departure from the divine right of kings in

Church and State to the present happy period of absolute political and religious freedom.

How much toward this great movement has been contributed by the eminent divines who have been pastors of this church, is a large part of the story to be told us to-day. If hero-worship is ever permissible, it is of these laborers for the truth and workers for salvation, whose spirits, we may fondly hope, join with us to-day in this renewed dedication of this sacred home of their highest earthly labors.

Let us, therefore, in this belief begin the ceremonies of the occasion with those venerable words of praise and prayer which for two hundred years have so comforted and strengthened the hearts of the children of men when gathered under this roof.

The Minister of the church then said : —

"The Lord is in His holy temple. Let all the earth keep silence before Him."

He also read, the congregation responding, Psalms xxiv., *Domini est terra;* lxxxiv., *Quam dilecta;* cxxii., *Lœtatus sum.*

Rev. FRANCIS GREENWOOD PEABODY, Plummer Professor of Christian Morals in Harvard University, then read the Scripture lesson from the eighth chapter of the First Book of the Kings, verses 12–18, 20, 22, 23, 26–30, 33–36, 54–60. After which the Minister of the church read collects and offered prayer.[1]

[1] In this part of the service he took the place of the Rev. FREDERICK AUGUSTUS FARLEY, D.D., of Brooklyn, N. Y., one of the oldest surviving children of the church, who was prevented from being present.

Minister. The Lord be with you.
Response. And with thy spirit.

Let us pray : —

LORD of all power and might, who art the author and giver of all good things; graft in our hearts the love of Thy name, increase in us true religion, nourish us with all goodness, and of Thy great mercy keep us in the same, through Jesus Christ our Lord.

O LORD, we beseech Thee mercifully to receive the prayers of Thy people who call upon Thee; and grant that they may both perceive and know what things they ought to do, and also may have grace and power faithfully to fulfil the same, through Jesus Christ our Lord.

O LORD, we beseech Thee to encourage the hearts of Thy faithful people, that they, always relying on Thy power and trusting in Thy grace, may bring forth plenteously the fruit of good works, and of Thee be plenteously rewarded, both in the world which now is, and that which is to come, through Jesus Christ our Lord.

O ALMIGHTY GOD, who hast knit together Thine elect, in one communion and fellowship, in the mystical body of the Son Christ our Lord; grant us grace so to follow Thy blessed saints in all virtuous and godly living, that we may come to those unspeakable joys which Thou hast prepared for those who unfeignedly love Thee, through Jesus Christ our Lord.

O GOD, who hast built the living temple of Thy Church upon the foundation of the Apostles and Prophets, Jesus Christ Himself being the chief Corner-stone; grant unto the work of Thine own hands continual increase of glory and spiritual strength, and daily make Thy people more meet for the eternal tabernacle of Thy rest in the heavens, through Jesus Christ our Lord.

ALMIGHTY and most merciful God, our Heavenly Father, gather us into the sanctuary of Thy holy presence, and fill our rejoicing with Divine joy and with the peace that passeth understanding. In the house that the fathers builded to Thee, the children's children still look to Thee for Thy faithful blessing, still trust in Thy continuing mercies, and pray in the Name which is above every name for Thy pardon and Thy peace.

We bless Thee for all pure and acceptable worship which has kindled its flame on this altar, for every faithful word of Thy servants, and every sacrifice of consecrated hearts. We praise Thee for the sure witness of one generation to another, testifying of Thy goodness and bearing the fruit of the gospel in lives renewed by Thy grace. Make us to be partakers with those who have gone before, in the great gift of the life immortal, and members of the Church of the first-born, whose names are written in heaven; and beyond this earthly tabernacle grant us to look for that building of God, the house not made with hands, eternal in the heavens.

For this church we invoke Thy consecrating Spirit, to renew it in the love and following of Thy blessed Son. We pray for the Church Universal, and for all who break to it the bread of life. At this time, as in duty bound, we pray for our Mother-Country and for her Queen; for this land and Commonwealth, and for those who are set over us in authority,— that rulers may rule in Thy fear, and that the hearts of Thy faithful people may be kept in godly quietness.

So grant that not alone the holy places where Thine honor dwelleth, but the wide earth may come to be none other than the house of God, the gate of heaven, and that all Thy children may pray the prayer of Our Lord Jesus Christ, —

OUR FATHER who art in heaven, Hallowed be Thy Name. Thy Kingdom come; Thy will be done on earth, as it is in heaven. Give us this day our daily bread. And forgive us our trespasses, as we forgive those who trespass against us. And lead us not into temptation, but deliver us from evil. For thine is the kingdom, and the power, and the glory, for ever and ever. Amen.

Then followed the giving out by Professor PEABODY and the singing of the version of Psalm lxxxiv. to "Winchester Tune," as it was in familiar use in the Church of England at the time of the foundation of King's Chapel, and was doubtless often sung here.

The Chairman then said: "The Rev. Henry W. Foote, the pastor of this church, needs no introduction at my hands. As the steward of the church, as the student of its history, as its official biographer, and still more as its loving child, no one could more confidently give us the interesting story of its past."

ADDRESS.

BY THE REV. HENRY WILDER FOOTE.

In this two hundredth year of our parish life, we welcome all who share its traditions. The present congregation, as the guardians to whom has been intrusted the duty of preserving and transmitting them, feel that these do not belong to themselves alone.

First of all, we reverently thank Almighty God, in this ancient house of prayer, that the angel of His presence has been with His people. While seven generations have come and gone like shadows, and all beside has changed around us, the breath of their piety lingers like incense, the light of God's illuminating answer still shines in His sanctuary. In this place which they of old time builded to His praise, we rise to the solemn elevation of those words of the Consecration Service which recognize that "devout and holy men, as well under the law as under the gospel, moved either by the express command of God or by the secret inspiration of the blessed spirit, . . . have erected houses for the public worship of God, and separated them from all unhallowed, worldly, and trivial uses, in order to fill men's minds with greater reverence for His glorious majesty, and affect their hearts with more devotion and humility in His service."

In accord with this high, reverent thought, these services seek to make clear to our sight different aspects of the divine leading in our past. So, then, we have not hesitated to bring into this Christian church these memorials, which revive again the memories once familiar here, — the royal governors, from Dudley to Hutchinson; the benefactors, like Peter Faneuil; the armorial bearings which formerly emblazoned these walls; and the banners of the colony and province of Massachusetts Bay which used to wave around this spot, and under which many a brave man went forth hence to the disasters of Martinique in 1693, and those of the St. Lawrence in 1711, or to the triumphs of Port Royal, and, later, of Louisburg and Quebec.

The two centuries bridge an interval which separates us from a world as remote as if it were mediæval, — the time of James Stuart in our mother land and church, of Louis XIV. in France. How shall we revive those ancient loyalties? In our age, so little sympathetic with the Old World life, and among a community founded by Puritans and indelibly marked with their strong impress, there is no slight danger of forgetting the generous elements which were inwrought into the fabric of New England history from the wealth and power of the mother-country, from the churchly habits and "sober standard of religious feeling" of men to whom their Book of Prayer was dear.

Children of the Puritans, indeed, most of us probably are. If any here are not, even they cannot escape from the fact that they are largely the mental and spiritual children of those masterful men. Nor should any religious commemoration in their good town of Boston fail to do honor to the faith for which they endured hardships, the consecrated will by which they tamed the wilderness, the clear and lofty purpose which shaped a community, perhaps more sober, steadfast, Bible-reading, Bible-loving than any other that the sun has ever shone upon, weaving together for fifty years a secure nest of religion and morals for a gentler form of faith to find shelter in. They were here, — the First Church, mother of the religious life of Boston, its character moulded by the saintly Wilson and the more potent spirit of Cotton; the Second Church, shepherded by the Mathers, and the Third by Willard. They gave no cheerful welcome, indeed, to the Church of England when it sought here a planting-ground and a place to take root in.

All passes before us in a swift succession of pictures as we gaze back. We see first the Rev. Robert Ratcliffe, Christian scholar and gentleman, with the little company around him of earnest churchmen on that fair day of May, 1686, when "worship, according to the use of the Church of England, is first had by authority in the town-house." We see the "12 formes for the servise of the church and the movable pulpit;" we hear the echo of the "prayers of ye church, to be said every Wednesday and Friday in the yeare, for the present, in the Library chamber in ye town-house in Boston, and in the Summer Season to beginne at 7 of the Clock in the morneing, and in the Winter Season at 9 of the Clock in the Forenoone." In August the first sacrament of the Church of England consecrates the town-house, that centre of the primitive Boston life, with an unsecular blessing. December brings Governor Andros, almost on this very day two hundred years ago; and few scenes are more vividly written for us in contemporary record than those in which the soldierly courtier from King James's court shines against the dark background of the Puritan divines. The reluctant hospitality of the South Meeting-house suffers rather than welcomes the new-comer. The gentle spirit of Lady Andros passes across the scene, and soon the "lychns illuminate the cloudy air as the bell tolls" for her burial. Then the wooden walls rise of the little church on a corner of the town's earliest burial-ground, where now we stand, and where it has been so long like a church of the Old World in its quiet churchyard.

The shadowy forms pass before us of the congregation who went in and out of that old church. But, as we gaze, these walls seem to shrink to narrower proportions; the pews are filled with worshippers whose faces still look forth as from the canvases of

Blackburn and Smibert; uniformed officers of the British Army and Navy brighten with scarlet the pew reserved for them; the finely decorated governor's pew holds stately guests. " In the west gallery is the first organ which ever pealed to the praises of God in this country, while displayed along its walls and suspended from its pillars, after the manner of foreign churches, are escutcheons and coats-of-arms; . . . in the pulpit an hour-glass, mounted on a large and elaborate stand of brass; and at the east end 'the altar-piece, whereon was the Glory painted, the Ten Commandments, the Lord's Prayer, the Creed, and some texts of Scripture.'" The tones echo faintly to our ear of the Rev. Samuel Myles, growing old in his ministry of thirty-nine years; of his successor, the Rev. Roger Price, rector and bishop's commissary with delegated Episcopal authority over the churches of his communion in New England; and of Caner, coming in his prime to the wooden church, soon to see his vision made real of this statelier building, to grow old in his ministry here, "the father of the American clergy," and to go forth an exile at the age of seventy-six years, loyal to his oath of allegiance to his king, with not a few of his congregation, when the darkening sky of the Revolution becomes night for them.

The scene changes. We see these solid walls rise, the first quarrying of that Quincy granite which the prudent builders were fearful lest they might exhaust. From far and wide come the contributions for its building; English cathedral clergy and London merchants, admirals like Sir Charles Knowles and Sir Peter Warren, Pepperell the victor of Louisburg, as well as bishops and the Crown itself, are asked for pious offerings. The people themselves pour forth — the rich of their treasure; the poor, of their mites — to rear what was meant to be the noblest house of worship in North America. Pre-eminent among them all as benefactors and founders of the new church shine the names of Shirley and Apthorp, whose monuments are fitly enshrined here. A noble organ, whose keys Händel's fingers are said to have touched, takes its place in the new church, and also a painting, said to be from the hand of Benjamin West. The altar gleams with silver plate, — the gift of three kings of England; and alternating with the successive rectors we hear the voices of the successive kings' lecturers, from Bridge to Troutbeck, whom the royal bounty sustains here as long as Church and State hold together. Meantime, a group of parishes of the Church of England have sprung up from this vigorous root, and Christ Church and Trinity Church as its children.

Through those ninety years, the central persons in the church are the governors who bear authority from the Crown, who mostly tread the way for worship between the Province House and the chapel of their king. These walls are draped in mourning for King George II., and hear the loyal prayer for his successor.

The scene again changes. The murmur of popular discontent grows louder. Trampling mobs pass near these walls, and Faneuil Hall and the South Meeting-house are not far away. That old world goes down in the earthquake of revolution; but the gray stone church still stands, though crown and mitre disappear. These aisles which have seen so many pageants enter, — one of the last in that loyal time the military funeral of Lieutenant-general Shirley, laid to rest in the vaults below, — now see the martyred Warren brought here from Bunker Hill, and hear the orator of that occasion first publicly utter in America the word "independence." Then follows the dramatic expiation to the Old South Church of its seizure by Governor Andros ninety years before, as it is kindly admitted here by the free consent of the wardens to hold its worship during more than five years of the war.

The scene changes yet once more, as we enter the modern chapter of the church's history, which has now endured for the last one hundred years. As its fragments knit together again, after being "torn from their king and church," changes come over its worship, larger even than the separation, yet with a great desire for truth and peace and Christian unity, and with a continuing love for the past, its religious associations, and its Christian faith. The church passes, with the new life of the time, from being the visible embodiment of the power and presence of the mother-country here, into the quiet religious ways of Christian duty and

JOSEPH DUDLEY.
(GOVERNOR 1702–1715.)

privilege, — one with a multitude of others here, all seeking in their several paths to make real the kingdom of God on earth.

Our commemoration to-day is not so much of this later time, but of the earlier, which has a universal interest, in which all may fitly claim a share. The latter days (in some of which we ourselves stand) tell their story in marble, — in part, by the busts of the godly ministers Freeman, Greenwood, and Peabody, and of a few of the many good men who have given this parish character in this community, and who would themselves have said that here they found the secret of what in them was best. We shall be stronger and better for remembering what manner of men these were; and this church, or any church, can ask no happier thing than that the children of such men may continue the worthy tradition of character and reverence and charity.

Nor did the latest period of our history pass without its being closely interwoven again in the great annals of the age. The revolution of 1689 saw the people led against Andros by John Nelson, his fellow-worshipper here; the revolution of 1776 saw the devoted loyalists go forth hence to exile, but the body of Warren brought here as the fittest place of honor; and it was twenty-five years last April since that martial music was heard once more, and Governor Andrew brought "tenderly" the Massachusetts soldiers who had fallen in the streets of Baltimore, and laid them to rest for a little space beneath this roof. The rest of the story is written in our hearts and on the western wall.

What remains but that we all, who ourselves remember with gratitude any touch of the divine Power that is over all our lives, here felt and known, or who know that the prayers of those whom we most honor in bygone generations have been filled from these ancient springs of faith that have "flowed fast by the oracle of God," should wish that with faith and power the old church may still lay hold of the new time; that the words of the old rector, when this corner-stone was laid, may be true to future generations as in the past: "Our worship is grave and comely, 'tis pure and simple, yet full of noble majesty, not superstitiously incumbered, nor indecently naked. Let every circumstance attending it partake of the same genuine and native ornament. Let the house of God in which it is performed rise up with the same majestic simplicity, neither incumbered with vain and trifling decorations, nor yet wanting in that native grandeur which becomes the beauty of worship, and which tends to beget impressions of awe and reverence in all that shall approach it." And that what was said by his successor a century ago may still be true: "Our earnest desire is to live in brotherly love and peace with all men, and especially with those who call themselves the disciples of Jesus Christ."

THE CHAIRMAN then said: "For nearly a century, the governors of the colony, in royal state, attended divine service in this church. The older members of the congregation can remember the high and ornamental pew set apart for their use. It was a picturesque addition to the architecture of the church. This pew, which was removed about sixty years ago, has been restored for this occasion ; and I am glad that the Governor of our Commonwealth, who honors us with his presence to-day, has been placed there as an expression of the respect, the gratitude, the affection which grace and dignify the closing days of his official life. If the people of Massachusetts had but one voice, they would say to him, with all the sincerity of truth and the solemnity of history, ' Well done, thou good and faithful servant ! ' We beg of his Excellency the favor of some words of sympathy."

ADDRESS.

BY GEORGE DEXTER ROBINSON, LL.D.,

Governor of Massachusetts.

AN occasion like the present brings the largest advantage when we are taught its lessons and suggestions. In the declaration of rights, the people of our Commonwealth have included the broad proposition that "all religious sects and denominations demeaning themselves peaceably and as good citizens of the Commonwealth shall be equally under the protection of the law; and no subordination of any one sect or denomination to another shall ever be established by law." So far as constitutional or legal provisions extend, every member of the body politic, protected against the domination of others, may choose his religious home with the body of worshippers he approves, and uphold his own household of faith as an essential and inalienable right.

The State is not constituted to teach religion; nor is the Church charged with the duty of making, expounding, or administering the civil laws. So broad is the separation between these momentous powers and privileges, so harmonious is the enjoyment of citizenship in Massachusetts, that we scarcely realize as we exclaim, " I was free born! " that the fathers obtained their freedom at a great cost and exceeding sacrifice, and bore many a grievous conflict to lay the foundations of civil and religious liberty on our soil upon so enduring a basis that its blessings far outnumber and surpass all the world has witnessed elsewhere.

It is abundantly fruitful, therefore, to recognize so important an anniversary as that you celebrate to-day, and to yield ourselves to the influence of the holy associations that cluster here.

We stand in the presence of the great past. We try to realize the situation, the exigencies, of the year 1686. We look forward a century, through perils and distress, and yet ever over heroism and invincible resolution, to the fruition of hope in the foundation of the Commonwealth and the adoption of the Constitution, and then down over another hundred years to the marvellous development and power exemplified in the present time. The very walls about us are eloquent beyond human speech. The ancient memorials tell the wonderful story. Again we seem to feel the inspiring presence of the noble men and women whose dust has long mingled with the soil whereon they trod, and whereon they reared sacred edifices and the still grander temple of universal freedom.

The Puritan had regarded the royal charter as his palladium. For fifty years it had been his refuge from oppression and wrong. Escaping from ecclesiastical tyranny in England, he was zealous in propagating in America his own system of faith, in crushing out every form of heresy, and in strengthening his church against the wicked assaults of its enemies. To hold fast to the faith, he maintained, assured life and strength; to tolerate liberality or indulgence toward another, yielded inevitably to death and hopeless ruin. He came to settle in America that he might enjoy the liberty of worshipping God according to the dictates of his own conscience, and he welcomed only those to equal privileges whose consciences worked in harmony with his own. Men of such mould and spirit were the first settlers of Boston.

We may well, then, conceive the horror and indignation with which, when the charter had been destroyed, the Puritan regarded the advent of Sir Edmund Andros, captain-general and governor-in-chief, glittering in scarlet and lace, and charged with the illegal and despotic commission from his sovereign king to force the establishment of the odious Church of England in Boston. Exclusive as was the Puritan himself, the act of the king and the bishops in overriding the wishes of the people and foisting upon them and into their own meeting-house the institutions they hated and resisted, was unjustifiable persecution and tyranny.

But the end we now see was sure to come. The grand destiny of the future overleaped the bounds the Puritan would place.

> "Himself from God he could not free;
> He builded better than he knew;
> The conscious stone to beauty grew."

Freedom for one became freedom for all. The way to the separation of Church and State was opened in Massachusetts. A hundred years later, explicit declaration was written into her constitution; and the union of the people in the grand republic of America was founded with the recognition of this providential and beneficent principle.

The storm had raged, the heavens had been overcast, the roar of the conflict had disturbed the land; but the broad resplendent sunshine that blesses us to-day fell all the more gratefully and benignantly upon the people who had endured the tempest and welcomed the glory of the brightening sky. Churches, sects, creeds, opinions — all and of every kind — are received in complete toleration. Through and over all is spread a warmer spirit of kindness and brotherly love, ministering in blessed charity to the down-trodden, the distressed, the broken-hearted; rearing splendid temples of beneficence that carry support and relief to the unfortunate, reformation to the vicious, instruction to the ignorant, and lifting this noble work far above the petty contentions of sectarian difference into the pure atmosphere of the gospel of Christ.

In so grand a position of power and beneficence does our beloved Commonwealth stand. I should be indeed faithless to her highest impulses and her heartfelt convictions did I not here and now recognize her obligation to the stern and godly men of yore, who built the ancient churches and gathered the people within their walls to worship God, to praise Him for His abundant blessings, and to invoke His great mercy and favor upon their undertaking in the cause of religion and liberty.

But the people of to-day cannot safely disregard their duty. If there shall be a great and honorable future, if the celebration of the next century's anniversary shall be crowned with renewed glory and continued peace and safety, it will be only because the sons hold in sacred trust what the fathers so grandly established and transmitted. The interests of religion lie near the life of the State. While the framers of our Constitution declared absolute toleration and protection for all forms of religious faith, they put them in union with unqualified recognition that "the public worship of God and instruction of piety, religion, and morality promote the happiness of the people and the security of a republican government." Though the State has no established church, her people cannot neglect the interests of religion without grave danger to good order and security. By no means have we any right to claim that it is a matter of no consequence whether public worship and religious teachings are maintained or not. That is not the guaranty from the past. Liberty is not license. Independence is by no means indifference. Privilege affords no release from duty.

Bitter, indeed, may be our scoffing and ridicule over the austerity and illiberality of the Puritan fathers; but merciless will be the condemnation coming generations will visit upon us, if while we boast of our freedom and flaunt our defiance of ecclesiastical control, ignorance, immorality, corruption, selfishness, and worldliness shall have despoiled us of our patrimony and blighted the prospects of the future. Bring religion and politics together into the domain of the private conscience; let the obligations a man owes to the public be tested by the standards of justice, of fairness, of integrity, of square dealing that characterize honorable intercourse among men, — in other words, carry the church, your church and mine, and the high inspirations that come from every religious communion, into public service and duty, and that union of Church and State, incarnating the noblest principles and the purest life, will bring no peril but rather unlimited support to our free institutions, and assure the stability of the State.

Says De Tocqueville: "Despotism may govern without religious faith, but liberty cannot. The United States must be religious to be free. Society must be destroyed unless the Christian moral tie be strengthened in proportion as the political tie is relaxed; and what can be done with a people who are their own masters, if they are not submissive to Deity?"

I am honored in the invitation to participate in the celebration of the establishment of this ancient church, and to it I respond in all the earnestness of my heart. No occasion like the present can pass without touching closely in sympathy all the people in Massachusetts. She abides to-day in her loyalty to the grand and noble deeds and sentiments of the past; and all the honor of her future rests in fidelity to God's eternal laws of justice, of holiness, of purity, and of uprightness, for which everywhere the true church shall be consecrated and revered in the hearts of men.

The original hymn by Dr. WILLIAM EVERETT, to the tune of St. Thomas, was then sung by the choir and congregation; after which the Chairman said: —

"The past of Massachusetts is rich with moral and intellectual wealth, of which this church has contributed its full share. We call on the President of the Massachusetts Historical Society to draw from the storehouse of his abundant knowledge the fruits of wisdom and instruction. Apart from our reverent relations to him as our frequent guide and teacher in the pulpit of this church, and as a member of the First Church of Boston, from which we welcome a voice of sympathy, there is a historical propriety in his presence and aid. The rooms of the Massachusetts Historical Society stand on the north side of our burial-ground, on the site of the home of the last provincial clergyman of this church, — the Rev. Dr. Caner, who at the

Revolution fled the country. This property was confiscated by the State, and eventually came into the possession of the Historical Society. In either building Dr. Ellis stands the representative and the exponent of the richest associations of our political and ecclesiastical history."

ADDRESS.

BY THE REV. GEORGE EDWARD ELLIS, D.D., LL.D.,

President of the Massachusetts Historical Society.

OUR local, historical, and memorial celebrations are becoming very numerous, as is realized by those privileged to take part in them. One of our New England mothers of a household, in the olden time of large families, began with a loving observance of the recurring birthdays of her children, as they came one by one or in pairs. But as they multiplied, so as to require a festive occasion almost in each month, she decided to take a general average of them, and to make the annual Thanksgiving Day a very happy one for them all. We may yet have to group some of our commemoration days.

But the first question to be asked of each of these occasions is as to what gives it its special interest, significance, or importance. So we ask of this occasion. And we distinguish at once between two elements in it, one of which we put all aside. The old feuds and rancors of religious controversy, the animosities and alienations attendant upon the planting of a church of the English model in a Puritan colony, are left by us to the past, — to history. As such, they have a full and impartial record on the admirably wrought pages of the first volume of the history of this Chapel by your present minister.

There is quite another point of view for our retrospect. Nature, as we see it in the old woods, gently covers with moss and creeping growths the wounded trunks and stumps in their decay. And so may picturesque incidents, touches, and fancies come to us as investing the exciting occasion when the English Church, with its observances, came uninvited here. As we look candidly at the facts, the time and occasion had rightfully matured for the recognition of the State religion of the realm on this peninsula. Even as the strife which was opened was the warmest, its incidents and features could not have been all grim and sour; some touches of merriment and humor must have relieved it. Whether that mischief-maker Randolph, in writing to the archbishop, used the word "lethargy" instead of "liturgy," as much needed here, or whether it was a mistake of the printer, the joke was equally an available one. We may trace the serious and the humorous incidents of the strife in the Diary of the good old Puritan judge Samuel Sewall, though what is humor to us was all very serious to him. Recall his deep sadness and his stiff resolve, when he was asked to sell a plot of his land on the ridge opposite this present building for a church. "No," said he, "the land belonged formerly to Mr. Cotton, the Non-Conformist exile from his mother-church. He would not wish his land to be used for such a purpose." That was reason enough. What a touch of home-life there is in the scene when his good little boy — afterward Dr. Joseph Sewall, of the Old South — wins his father's approbation by telling him that he had not been beguiled by his playmates to peep into the Chapel for a sight of the Christmas decorations! Or mark the satisfaction of the judge himself, as he counts the teams of hay and wood that come into the town and the shops open, though it be Christmas Day.

Recall vividly and calmly the historic incident of the beginning here. This wilderness peninsula had been reclaimed for peaceful and thrifty English homes, through hard toil for fifty-six years, by the zeal and manfulness of English exiles, who, oppressed by a class of bishops quite unlike those known to us, — temporal as well as spiritual lords, with their prerogatives and courts, — had sought a refuge here. The exiles had memories and smarts and sturdy principles. They set up worship and methods of their own. Those who had been brought here as little children, and a new generation from their stock, had grown into active life on the as yet rude stage. Nursed and nurtured amid rough stern scenes, under a parental Puritanism, this new generation, without the gentle and gracious memories of their fathers of the dear old English home, had stiffened into more hardness and rigor in their religion. The tables were to be turned here, exactly inverting the relations between Puritans and

MRS. REBECCA (TYNG) DUDLEY.

(WIFE OF GOVERNOR JOSEPH DUDLEY.)

Churchmen in England. Puritanism was our established church; Churchmen were dissenters. But the shock came. The surpliced priest, and soon his "box of whistles" to help out native psalmody, his read prayers, his changing attitudes in worship, his saints' days, including that for the "holy martyr Charles I.," who belonged to quite another fellowship for the Puritans, — all these came; and they brought consternation with them. But they came rightfully and opportunely. There was a constituency and material here for an English church. It was a critical and transitional period for the Puritan commonwealth. The colony charter had been vacated; and the Crown had strongly asserted its prerogatives here, with new organic rules, backed by its official emissaries. There were here sworn servants of the monarch, officers of the customs, of the army and the navy, coming and going in the military operations of the time. The portraits and insignia, which for this occasion adorn this edifice; the tablet of the royal arms, once attached to the house of the royal governor, now suspended before me, — are all emblems to us, so out of place for a Puritan meeting-house, of residents here who desired their own place and form of worship. Besides these, it is to be remembered, were inhabitants engaged in commerce and trade, who had not severed their ties of love and loyalty to the mother-country. And yet, further, there were here not a few native born, alienated from the doctrine and discipline of Puritanism, who could not comply with the exacted conditions of baptism for their children or with the terms of admission to the communion. Many of these sought the milder ways of the English Church. It was on such as these last that Judge Sewall kept a watchful eye. It grieved him to hear of the tolling church-bell or the reading of the solemn burial-service over some who he thought had not died in the odor of sanctity.

Rightfully, as I have said, was the Church of England planted in this town. Of course, it caused grief and anxiety here to others than those who were rigid in bigotry. We may well believe that there were many of clear, vigorous, mental powers and of a generous spirit, who saw in this recognition of the royal presence and sovereignty in a privileged State church the tightening of a foreign power over a previously independent people. It was a sign, and they dreaded what might come of it. The displeasure natural here was greatly imbittered by some arbitrary and offensive acts of the royal governor. He acted on the assumption that the town and people were bound to provide him with a place and aids in his worship. He so appropriated the South Church against the remonstrances, and to the annoyance and discomfort, of its proprietors. The times were then distracted. Important public papers and records are lost. It does not appear by what method, whether of purchase or allowance from the town or by seizure, Andros planted the edifice preceding this on the corner of the first burial-ground of Boston.

That wooden and this precious stone edifice served the purpose of the Church of England for nearly ninety years. The "King's Lecturer," whose presence gave dignity to the ministrations at the Royal Chapel, received his stipend from the Crown. The resources of the congregation provided for the associate rector, and for the current expenses. Then came the war of the Revolution, extinguishing the royal power in our land. The rector of the Chapel and a large portion of his loyal flock, the proprietors of this edifice, left the country, never to come back again. The edifice escaped destruction or insult from the returning inhabitants after the siege, though they were smarting under the demolition of one and the defilement of three other of their sanctuaries.

The South Church, now standing at the corner of Milk Street, had been so wrecked and polluted by the British soldiers that it was only after five years that its impoverished owners were able to cleanse and restore it. In the interval, the congregation worshipped in this deserted Chapel; and here their minister, Rev. Dr. Eckley, was ordained. Of what followed here — the consequent dropping away from the English Church, the change in the renewal of the ministry and in your ritual for worship — you will soon have an exhaustive, candid, impartial, and interesting narration in the second volume of the historical work by your minister. The remnant left of the old proprietors of the edifice, joined by others, renewed here much of the previous form of worship. But the liturgical books in pews and reading-desk were no longer serviceable. The young man, James Freeman, who was invited here as reader and preacher, objected not only to the prayers for the King of England, but to the forms of addressing the King of kings. There was then no organized Protestant Episcopal Church in the United States, and ordination by its ritual could not be obtained here for ministers. There was much confusion and variance of opinion over the whole country on the subject. The rector of Christ Church in Philadelphia, afterward the beloved and venerated Bishop White, with some associates, had proposed a method for the continuance of his communion in this country without help from English bishops, and had also prepared a book as a proposed manual for worship, which afterward received but slight respect. The changes made in the Book of Common Prayer for use in this Chapel were made deliberately and conscientiously. The most important of them were the omission of terms of speech, words, phrases, and sentences which were not drawn from the Scriptures, and the substitution for them of those more strictly Scriptural. All sacerdotal, hierarchical, and ecclesiastical elements were also eliminated from the pages of the book. It is for those who are to follow me to retrace the later history of the congregation, and to commemorate its ministers.

I have been asked to say a few words about Dr. Greenwood. Most gladly do I do so. Of all the loved and venerated men who now in thickening fellowship gather about my memory, there was no one of a more saintly, apostolic, grave loveliness, dignity, and beauty than Dr. Greenwood. Pardon me if my reference to him is personal. I recall him when he was just closing his first ministry at the New South Church in Summer Street, — a delicate, frail man, seeming to have but a short tenure of life, afflicted with that pulmonary weakness which followed him through his whole course. I was at the age of five years. I distinctly remember him, as after being housed through the whole winter he came out to his meeting-house, and, unable to climb the stairs of the pulpit, stood by the communion table and read a brief letter of thanks to his congregation for their kindness in having furnished him the means of foreign travel. His beloved physician, the venerated and endeared Dr. Jackson, had pronounced him in such a condition that even if his life were prolonged he would never preach again. On leaving that service he stopped at my father's house, a few doors from the church, and there baptized a little infant, the late minister of the First Church in Boston. I recall one of those philosophical discussions in the nursery after that occasion, such as will take place among children, — when we debated the question whether one would rather be that little infant, who had the prospect of a long and happy life, or that poor sick, frail minister who seemed so near the grave; and we concluded that it would be better to be the minister, for he was so good that he was sure to go right to heaven as an angel the moment he died.

Years passed, and Dr. Greenwood as your minister lived to exchange pulpits at Northampton with that little infant!

Fifty years ago this month, I stood for the first time in this pulpit to help Dr. Greenwood in his infirmity; and here, before I had a charge of my own, I preached for several weeks and months while he was absent through the winter at Santa Cruz. I had frequent opportunities of intimacy with his sweet and lovely spirit and character. The tones of his voice were almost a sermon and a prayer. And perhaps I express the feeling of many, or of some at least who remember him here, when I repeat an anecdote. As I had been preaching here one Sunday during his absence, on passing out of the aisle I was with the late Charles P. Curtis, who I think was then an officer of the church. He pronounced a few kind words about my youthful performance; but he added, "I would rather hear Dr. Greenwood preach the same sermon every Sunday in the year than hear anybody else in the pulpit."

THE MINISTER then said: "It has been recalled to you how peculiarly the history of this church and that of one of the Puritan churches of this city have been connected in the past, at the beginning of the two centuries. Again, midway in their course, the Old South Church and King's Chapel had special relations. It is peculiarly fit, therefore, that at the beginning of our third century the minister of the Old South should speak to us."

ADDRESS.

BY THE REV. GEORGE ANGIER GORDON,
Minister of the Old South Church.

THE history of the connection of King's Chapel and the Old South Church is very interesting indeed. It has been necessarily anticipated by the speakers who have preceded me, but it is interesting enough for me to call your attention to it again.

King's Chapel, like most other churches, was born poor. It came into the world before it had an ecclesiastical home. It organized itself into a church before it had a place wherein to worship. In May of 1686 the first minister came to Boston, and during that summer and fall and winter of 1686 and 1687, as you have been told, the congregation worshipped in the library of the town-house. That bare and meagre room did not seem quite consonant with the dignity and magnificence of the Episcopal service. What was to be done? To build they were not able, but to beg they were not ashamed. There were then three flourishing Congregational churches in Boston, — the First, Second, and the Third, or what is now known as the Old South. The Old South, or the Third Church, had the best meeting-house, and was situated in the best part of the town, which the royal Episcopal governor was not slow to appreciate. So he sent a request to the proprietors of the Old South Meeting-house for permission to hold service in that edifice, and an order to adjust all their services to suit his convenience. Both request and order were stoutly opposed. The demand was made again and again, but met with the same response. Finally, the Governor marched to the church at the head of a party; and although the sexton had given his word that he would grant no admission, nevertheless he did, and rang the bell. It was in March, 1687, when the Governor and his party entered the church; and for about two years they maintained joint occupancy of the Old South Meeting-house with the regular proprietors of the church. Now, the sum of this connection seems to be that King's Chapel was poor; it was not to blame for that. It wanted a good meeting-house; it was not to blame for that. It gave the preference to the Old South; it was not to blame for that. But when it came to securing admission by force, and maintaining its standing by force, it seems to me that it was somewhat to blame for that.

The second incident in the connection of the two churches, perhaps, you will be more pleased to hear of. During the siege of Boston, in 1775, as you all know, the meeting-house of the Old South Church was applied to base uses. The congregation was turned out; and their pastor, Rev. Mr. Hunt, left the city for Northampton, where he died in December. This was, indeed, a sad time for the Old South congregation. They were without a meeting-house, and without a pastor. They were turned into the street, and were homeless wanderers. The organization was kept intact by a few resolute, devout, faithful men; and in the hour of their extremity King's Chapel, with Christian hospitality and with the most delightful feeling of fraternity, opened her doors and bade them welcome to hold service within the walls of this edifice. The offer was gladly accepted; and Mr. Joseph Eckley, then preaching in town, was asked to preach to the Old South congregation. Their first service was held here Nov. 9, 1777; and for a period of five years, with one interruption, the Old South congregation continued to worship in this edifice. In 1779, Mr. Joseph Eckley was here ordained as minister of the Third Church, and continued to serve that church acceptably for over thirty years. Nothing is known of this service of ordination; if any one has any records of it, or information concerning it, they will be gladly received by the Old South Church. You will see, if the first incident stands somewhat to the dishonor of King's Chapel, the second, in its enduring Christian fraternity, is more than an offset to the arrogance of the first.

Now, this historical little sermon seems to have an application to the two congregations. The first is this: If ever King's Chapel should become poor again, if it should ever lose its meeting-house, if it should ever look abroad among the churches of this city for a temporary home, and if it should again give preference to the Old South, why that would seem very natural to us; and if it should come in the bland and insinuating manner of these modern days and ask for admission, I have no doubt the society and the sexton would be very accommodating. But if it should come in the manner of the ancient time, I am afraid that the success which it had in 1687 would not be repeated in 1887. This is the first point.

The second is this: The Old South cherishes the expectation that if a body of men should again desecrate and dishonor its meeting-house and turn its congregation into the street, and if it should lose its pastor, King's Chapel would generously open its doors again. If a pastor were to be ordained and installed, and a contentious Orthodox ecclesiastical council to be entertained, the Old South still cherishes the hope that the hospitality and forbearance of King's Chapel would again be found equal to the emergency.

The version of Psalm xxiii., by Rev. Cotton Mather, was then sung to "York Tune," after which the Minister said: "The President of Harvard University stands officially in close relations with the churches of Massachusetts historically, pre-eminently so with the churches of the city of Boston; and of those churches, none perhaps is more closely related than this to the University in the number of students it has furnished thereto, and of graduates it has received back during these two hundred years. But in coming to King's Chapel, the President of Harvard University is coming home to the church which his father served, to the church of his own youth; and on this historic occasion it may be permitted me to add, that he comes in the sixth generation from ancestors whose portraits hang on these walls to-day, being in that degree of descent from Governor Joseph Dudley."

ADDRESS.

BY CHARLES WILLIAM ELIOT, LL.D.,
President of Harvard University.

IT seems to me that we should speak of this church to-day as something more than an historical monument. To many of us it has been a living and a working church. I will say a few words to you, simply as a son of this church.

This place is full of touching memories for me, and I doubt not for many others here present who were brought up in this church, but who have been separated from it in after life because their homes or their occupations were at a distance. When we children of the church return, we can hardly see the people that are actually before us, so distinct is our vision of the young men and maidens, the old men and children, who sat in these pews when we were young. We can hardly hear the choir of to-day for listening to familiar voices of other days, hushed long ago. From this desk there speaks to us a deep, solemn monotone which thrilled the listener's ear forty years since. Up this aisle there come processions very plain to memory's sight, some joyous and some mournful, coming to wedding, to christening, or to funeral; and in these companies of kindred and friends we look with a kind of compassionate interest upon our former selves. We stand aside as it were for a moment and witness the passing by of the generation to which we belong, — the extinction of the former generation, and the oncoming of the succeeding.

We think very tenderly of these consecrated walls, as if they had some tender benediction to shed upon the baptisms, betrothals, marriages, burials, which have marked here for us the chief events in our family lives. And then we remember that seven generations have had these same precious associations with this ancient church, and find our imaginations unable to picture the smiles and tears, the happiness and grief, its two houses on this spot have witnessed.

There are more public grounds for cherishing kindly thoughts of the families who in the earlier generations worshipped God in this place. As has been called to our attention this afternoon, they were largely loyalists as well as devoted members of the Anglican Church. Now, the total loss of any cause which men and women have served with passionate loyalty is always pathetic. The loyalists got hard measure in the Revolution. Many of them suffered exile and the confiscation of their property, only to find the coldest of welcomes in the mother-country or in the still loyal provinces. On this consecrated ground, after the lapse of a century, we Republicans cannot help sympathizing with the distress and personal sorrow which the long-continued peril and final overthrow of the royalist cause brought to many a King's Chapel family. Moreover, we perceive that our modern Republican loyalty to that personified ideal which we call our

WILLIAM BURNET.

(Governor 1728, 1729.)

country is a virtue close akin to the older loyalty to idealized personages — to kings, queens, and princes — which the families connected with this church illustrated in the midst of an unsympathetic community.

Finally, the conservatism of this church makes her scattered children very tender toward her; for when they return to her at rare intervals they find her unchanged. Religious opinions and practices may have undergone rapid transformations in the outer world; we who have been separated from the old church may have changed our own views; but we come back hither to find the harbor just as we left it, and as our fathers knew it. The world could not spare its adventurers and pioneers; but for one pioneer it needs a thousand conservers, in order that all the good the past has won or the present wins may be held fast and safely transmitted. As a rule, the conserver is more lovable than the critic or the pioneer. This church is a conserver.

THE MINISTER then said: "The great communion of the Episcopal Church in America has its share in these traditions, and its members are partakers in the early memories of this Chapel. It was therefore hoped that it might have been possible for the Right Reverend Bishop of the Protestant Episcopal Diocese of Massachusetts to be with us to-day as its official head; but his official engagements have called him elsewhere. The rector of Trinity Church, who will now speak to us, comes not alone as the representative of that communion, but as the minister of a church which sprang from this in the early days."

ADDRESS.

BY THE REV. PHILLIPS BROOKS, D.D.,
Rector of Trinity Church.

During the past seventeen years I have owed a great many of the pleasures which I have enjoyed to my connection with Trinity Church. I owe the privilege of being here to-day, and the fact that I am the rector of that church, to a certain scene which took place on a bright April morning in the year 1734, when Mr. Commissary Price, who was then rector of King's Chapel, went down to the corner of Summer Street and Bishop's Alley and laid the corner-stone of Trinity Church. One year after that time, at the same place, in the building which had been erected during the year, the services of Trinity Church were inaugurated by a service held and a sermon preached by the same Mr. Commissary Price; and the life of the new church at once began, under the rectorship of Rev. Addington Davenport, who up to that time had been in some way associated with the services in King's Chapel, but who then became the first minister of Trinity Church. And so our histories are bound together.

Mr. Davenport is now to us a very dim and misty person, but everything that we learn of him is altogether to his credit; and he gave at once to the services that were held at Trinity Church and to that new parish a very dignified and honorable position. He stands to us now mainly as a link to connect the lives of the two parishes, and to let us feel that we belong to the same line of succession to which the parishioners of King's Chapel belong.

When one has a happy life, he feels thankful to those who gave him a chance to live that life. And when a parish has lived the happy life which Trinity Church has lived, while trying in its way and time to do some useful work, it is thankful to those who gave it the beginning of its existence and the opportunity to do that work; and so we are thankful to those from whom you sprang, and from whom we sprang, that they founded Trinity Church in that year 1734.

I have tried to think what is the real relationship between the King's Chapel of to-day and the Trinity Church to which you have given your invitation. It is not easy to fasten it. It is not simply that you are the mother-church and we are the daughter-church. It is something like the relation which has come to exist between the life of our own country and the life of the England across the seas. We talk in a pleasant way about England being the mother-country and of this country of ours being the daughter-country; but when we come to examine this and to study the relationship, we find that we have not stated it exactly as it is. The England of to-day is not the mother of which the United States is the daughter. The England of to-day and the United States of America are sister nations; and the mother of us both lies two centuries back, — in the rich life of the seventeenth century, out of which we and so much of the best of English life have sprung. England is the daughter who has remained at home; we are the daughter who has gone abroad. We are not her daughter, and she is not our mother.

So it is — is it not? — with reference to the relation which exists between your parish and the parish which I have the pleasure of representing. We are both the children of that peculiar English life — the life of the English Church transported to this land and planted here — which has been so felicitously described to us this afternoon. You are daughters of that history; we are daughters of that history, not of a daughter parish.

Let us look for a moment on the face of our mother. She does not shine in the history of America. The attempt to establish the English Church in the colony of Massachusetts in those older days was not a successful, happy, nor shining part of our history; and yet I am sure that there was something that passed from it into the mental, ecclesiastical, social, and perhaps even the political life of America which it would be a pity to have lost. Our mother, the English Church, trying to establish herself in the colonies, came somewhat awkwardly, as might have been expected. She tried to plant herself in the midst of an antagonism that made her awkward and ungraceful in her coming. But she did bring with her something of that profound reverence for the past, something of that deep sense of religious order, something which she had clung to as the true form of devotion, something which had all the respectability of form and communion which characterized the life of the English Church throughout her history and experience in the old land. The trouble was that she came and remained a foreigner; and just as soon as the foreigner was no longer to be tolerated, she passed out of the life which had been gradually acquiring its own national character. The beauty of her life was that these two children she left behind — King's Chapel and Trinity Church — were thoroughly American, in spite of her old associations and her unfortunate life in a foreign land. She stamped upon those two congregations a distinctively American character. I do not learn — though those who are wiser than I am may correct me — that the congregation of King's Chapel was largely broken up by that exodus in which the rector of King's Chapel departed, carrying so much with him that was representative of her history. Certainly the body of the congregation remained, and perpetuated the life which has resulted in the history which has come from that day to this. And I do feel proud that the congregation of Trinity was the only congregation of the Episcopal Church anywhere in this neigborhood which did so deeply retain association with the life of the colonies and the cause with which they were identified that she had their spirit of independence, that she preserved her service throughout the whole of the Revolutionary War, and that she formed the nucleus around which the life of the Episcopal Church was gathered after the war had closed.

So our mother the English Church at least succeeded in this, that she made others American, if she did not become American herself. She succeeded in inspiring that spirit which must always be cherished, — that while the great Christian faith is one everywhere throughout the world, it is one part of Christian duty, and must be one element of a church's successful life, to identify herself with the national life in the midst of which she lives; that she shall sympathize with every national misfortune and wrong, and shall always be ready to rejoice in the progress of true usefulness and the larger happiness of the nation in which she belongs.

I congratulate King's Chapel that its history has been a patriotic history from the beginning to the end. There was no lack of patriotism so long as she sprang from and associated herself with the life of the colonies in the days of the Revolution. From that time she has had her typical men among the noblest, purest, holiest in our American pulpit. She has been ever ready to catch the spirit of every new cause, — not rash of impulse, not throwing herself into the stream of every enthusiasm of the hour, but always ready to sympathize deeply with every wrong of the land, and to help every right which was striving for assertion. And when the great crisis of our history came, she sent her young men, — none nobler, none more numerous, from any city or country congregation, — she sent her young men into the field; and there they bore testimony to the life which they had learned to live here at home.

It is a great thing for a church thus to have been associated with a nation's life, — always ready to meet each new emergency which called it to its work, always ready to be even a little beforehand by a general recognition of that which was coming, and by preparing her children by the fundamental teaching of righteousness and truth that they should be ready when the time arrived.

One looks back over this history of two hundred years; and it is full of such associations as this, — the imagination has so much room to wander in! One of the things to rejoice in on a great occasion like this is that this Chapel has stood for two centuries, imbibing such a multitude of personal experiences, representing such countless souls that have passed out of the world of living men and women and are now with God; that she has striven with issues, some of which have been settled, and others which have developed into larger issues, which have claimed in their turn the souls of men; that she has stood, generation after generation, for the simplicity, the dignity, the majesty, and the worth of the Christian religion and the Christian ministry; that she has had such men in her pulpit, men full of the spirit of Christian faith, righteousness, and love; men who, to the congregation which listened to them, have represented something more than the truth they preached, — the dignity of Christian manhood and the sweetness of human character. It is a great thing that a pulpit should represent, not simply a gospel, but a man; not merely a truth, but a character; not merely doctrines which people are to believe, but also a ministry which should gain the respect of young men generation after generation; that it should teach men to believe the truth that the Christian ministry is indeed the noblest occupation, the grandest profession, in which men can engage. When the time shall come, as it certainly will come, that young men shall know that truth; when there shall run through our schools and colleges a new perception, that, great as are the glories which belong to other occupations, — and I would not undervalue them, — there is none that can compare with those attaching to the preaching of the gospel to the children of God, — then the voices that have thrilled from the pulpit of the King's Chapel shall have a testimony to bear which shall deepen the impression of that truth as it comes home to the minds of young men. It shall bear testimony to the way in which that truth has been gloriously manifested in the lives and characters and speaking experiences of those men who have stood here; who from the very fact of being here have preached the nobleness of life, the richness of the pursuit of truth, the worthlessness of everything that does not somehow fasten itself to the law of God, the brotherhood of mankind, and the assurance of a universal Fatherhood.

One of the beauties of such a day as this is that

it takes up a long history, and gathers it together within the embrace of great principles. History develops itself here and there in a vast multitude of incidents and in scattered ways. These commemorative days take the multitude of the events of history and gather them up together, and enfold them in the great principles which have been ruling through them all, and in which they must all find their explanation.

It has been intimated here this afternoon that the history of King's Chapel has been a varied one; that men have differed in opinion; that there have been discussion and dispute. It would not be a true picture of the thinking Christian world if it had been otherwise. It would not have been a true life of the Church if it had not represented men differing from other men with reference to the things which belong, not to the surface, but to the very depth and substance of our faith. Let us set ourselves, friends, — we who belong to the common Church of Christ, — let us set ourselves against the false teaching of the times that would disparage theology. Let us set ourselves against the false sentiment that would speak of theological discussion as if it were a thing of the past, a blunder in its day, and something which the world has outgrown. When the world ceases to theologize, — to seek for the deepest and inmost truth with regard to the innermost nature of God, — there has fallen a palsy upon it. Let us rejoice that the history of this church represents the thought of earnest men who have again and again differed from one another because they have thought and felt deeply about divine things. God has never left the minds of his children unstirred. But while they have differed from one another, let us rejoice in this, — that we are looking back upon the history of men who were earnestly seeking after truth. And as that history gathers itself into our Christian consciousness to-day, let us rejoice that it lets us believe that God has vaster purposes in the history of this and of all his churches than those who have worked faithfully on these problems are able to understand. Who believes to-day that the things which took place in the beginning of this century have come to a final result? Who believes that the changes which took place in connection with this church and its re-formation at the close of the Revolutionary War have come to their final culmination? Who does not feel, as he stands at the close of these two hundred years and looks back upon the past, the necessity of believing that God out of these many years will bring rich results in the future; that the problems which have been reasoned have not yet been solved? Who is not ready to rejoice in every disturbance of the past, so far as it has been the work of good and earnest men striving to get at the truth of God and Jesus Christ?

How shall we prepare ourselves for that future? Not by reviving old disputes, but by recognizing the earnestness which entered into those disputes, — by consecrating ourselves in personal obedience to that Christ whose nature, earnestly studied, has led men apart from one another, as they have tried to understand that which is beyond the understanding of men only because it is infinite and cannot be reached by their intelligence, not because it is denied to their study by any wall of prohibition. It seems to me that any one who looks back on the past and recognizes in history the great providence of God in his dealings with men, — so much deeper than men have begun to comprehend, — simply wants to say to any church, speaking for his own as he speaks for others: Let us go and seek that Christ, that infinite Christ, whom we have not begun to know as we may know him, — that Christ who has so much more to show us than he has shown; that Christ who can show himself to us only as we give ourselves in absolute obedience to him. May that Christ receive from us, in each new period of our history, more complete consecration, more entire acceptance of him as our Master; and so may we receive from him rich promises of new light, new manifestations of his truth, new gifts of his spirit, which he has promised to bestow upon those who consecrate themselves to him in loving obedience, unto the end of time and through all eternity! If one may turn a greeting to a prayer, may I not ask for you, as I know you ask for all of our churches, a more profound and absolute spirit of consecration to our master Christ, that in him, and only in him, we may seek after and come to his ever richer life?

The Magnificat in F, by B. Tours, was then sung; after which the Minister said: "There is one name which to the members of this congregation who are now in middle life or beyond it, will always be that of the minister of this church. Of him, one who has a special right, as the friend most closely associated with him in his Christian ministry, will now speak to us."

ADDRESS.

BY THE REV. JOHN HOPKINS MORISON, D.D.

The transition from Dr. Greenwood to Dr. Peabody was an easy one, the apostolic succession being unbroken in the change from one saintly man to another.

Forty years ago there was no one in our little fraternity who was more universally loved by his brethren, or looked up to with a more happy and confiding trust than Ephraim Peabody. One could hardly be with him, even for a little time, without feeling that here was a man absolutely honest and truthful. There was something about him which at first, and then more and more as we knew him better, gave us a sense of largeness, — of a man made on a large scale, and from his very constitution incapable of lending himself to anything small. The bare suggestion of such a thing could find no place — not even a hiding-place — in his pure and generous mind. In connection with this largeness was a delicacy of perception, which made him peculiarly sensitive to the finer influences of nature and

JONATHAN BELCHER.

(Governor 1730-1741.)

society; which enabled him to read intuitively the characters of men around him as in a book, and which brought him into the closest sympathy with what is finest in literature, and above all with what is most tender, far-reaching, and inspiring in the life and teachings of our Saviour. These great qualities showed themselves especially in the faculty of entering into the condition and needs of others with a wisdom which can come only from above, and which then can be applied only by the watchful care and insight that are prompted by unselfish sympathies and affections. These were the dominant features in the character of our friend.

In his early preaching, an occasional hearer might at first recognize only the style of thought and expression which came to him with his Puritan birth and training, and which might give the impression of a persistent and merciless severity. But as he goes on, the hard tones of the preacher melt into pathos. An unspeakable tenderness pervades his whole nature, as he places before his hearers images of moral danger, of Christian faith and love, of patience under suffering, or of hope in death, which touch every heart, and sometimes seem almost to suspend the breathing of the audience as they listen tearfully to his words.

Later in life he changed this mode of preaching. "I have got tired," he said, "of rhetoric even in speeches. The truth! We have got finally to stand upon it; and I thank no man for trying to glorify or hide it by his rhetoric." With this conviction growing upon him, he gradually gave up the pictorial illustrations which he had employed with a faculty for word-painting in which he was surpassed, so far as I know, by no preacher since the days of Jeremy Taylor. The consequence was that in his later sermons his imagination showed itself less in separate and extended illustrations, and infused its coloring more, like the veins of some beautiful marble, through the entire fabric. In reading them, we seem at times to be brought once more within the charm of that genial, diffusive nature which spread itself out over those who were with him like a summer's day. The mellowness of his ripening affections, his calmer wisdom, and richer thought gave tone and character alike to his private conversation and his public instructions. Compared with his former writings, his later sermons are marked by a severer taste, and at the same time a greater freedom of expression. We feel as we go on the all-pervading presence of a more comprehensive wisdom, a greater depth and freshness of feeling, a more subdued solemnity and tenderness, an imagination enriched by the studies and experiences of life, and working as a vitalizing energy through the whole living texture of his thought.

And as his preaching, such also was the man. Truthfulness, absolute truthfulness, was the controlling principle of his being. This alone could satisfy either his mind or his heart. This truthfulness of soul in its elevation and expansiveness bore him up, and opened before him a sphere in which he found room for the exercise and free play of all the faculties with which he had been so largely endowed.

I cannot think of him without having uppermost in my mind a sense of largeness of nature, and, inseparably connected with this, a certain fineness of texture running through his whole intellectual, moral, and emotional being. These two qualities of largeness and delicacy, with the attributes which of necessity go with them in a nature so finely and liberally endowed, are the surest tokens of greatness, as they reveal themselves in a man's daily conduct and in the great opportunities and crises of life. It has been my privilege to know many of the great men, many of the most thoroughly consecrated and self-sacrificing, of all who during the last fifty years have helped to make this community what it is. Some of these men have been known and honored throughout the world, and some have been hardly known beyond the little neighborhood in which their lot was cast. But among them all, I call to mind no one who could better bear the test of greatness here suggested than the modest pastor who "in simplicity and godly sincerity" ministered at this altar, and died a few days more than thirty years ago. Not as the world judges, I know, but in the elements of true greatness as illustrated by our great Teacher, I have known no greater man than he. In the largeness and fineness which pervaded all his faculties and made them what they were; in the "sound wisdom" which goes so deep and reaches so far; in the ruling motives of conduct, and in the sympathies and affections which "void of offence towards God and man" give breadth and sweetness, and throw around one an unnamed but irresistible attractiveness and charm, — I have known no greater man than he.

There is no time now to prove what I have said by the analysis of what our friend was as shown in his acts and words. But lest it should seem the extravagance of a partisan or a personal friend, I give the testimony of a very able man, who belongs to a different profession and a different branch of the church, and who never heard Dr. Peabody preach, but who knew him well for many years, and at times was brought into very intimate relations with him. After speaking of some of his remarkable traits, especially, as he says, "the keenest insight into character I ever knew," so that "his estimate of men was almost infallible," he adds; "Of all the men I ever knew, he was the one from whom I learned the most on questions of conduct, who impressed me most powerfully by his remarks on the mysteries and trials of life, and from whom I got the most aid in trouble, and the most light in the difficult pathways which are common to all."

This comes from one who had known him long and well in the more private and personal relations. To those who thus met him alone in his confidential moments, there was something very deep and very uplifting and inspiring. The great things of this world become of small account. We are taken up into a higher realm. We see in him an expression of reverence and of loving trust such as sometimes settles down on the face of a thoughtful child. We feel ourselves compassed about by a diviner order. It is as if we had been brought before Him who, when his disciples had been disputing who should be greatest among them, "called unto him a little child and set him in the midst of them." And from the lips of the great Master we seem to hear and to understand as never before the words, " For of such is the kingdom of heaven."

THE MINISTER then said: "Before we join in singing the hymn which has been written for this occasion by our friend and fellow-worshipper, it will be read by one who has an ancestral claim to share in this service, — the grandson and namesake of the Warden who for more than fifty years gave this church a loyal service exceeding that of any other single member of the parish in the long line, and whose monument is on these walls, — Colonel Joseph May. And then the minister by whose side Colonel May stood from youth to age, — from the time when the young Reader came here as yonder portrait represents him, to the venerable years which his bust indicates, — whose more than half a century in this church has left a fresh and imperishable impress, will speak again to this people by the filial lips of Dr. James Freeman Clarke."

The original hymn by Dr. Oliver Wendell Holmes was then read by the Rev. Joseph May, of Philadelphia, and sung to the tune of Tallis' Evening Hymn by the congregation, after which followed the

ADDRESS.

BY THE REV. JAMES FREEMAN CLARKE, D.D.,
Minister of the Church of the Disciples, Boston.

TWICE in my life I have seen this Chapel as full as it is to-day. Once was a great while ago, after the declaration of peace with Great Britain. I cannot pretend to remember much; but I do remember, as a little boy, being very much surprised by seeing so many people in this building, and by seeing such an extended choir on each side of the organ. The other occasion was when Edward Everett returned from Europe, and Dr. Freeman — who had a talent for discovering genius and ability in young men, and a great admiration of genius and ability wherever it was found — asked him to preach in this pulpit on Christmas Day; and not only was every seat full, but this middle aisle was filled with people standing. Dr. Freeman admired Buckminster, he admired Dr. Channing, he admired James Walker, — all men younger than himself, — and was very fond of having them here.

But it is, perhaps, a privilege which belongs to me, to remember a few of those shadowy forms whom our friend President Eliot spoke of as coming before his eyes. In the Governor's pew, when it was as you have rearranged it to-day, before it had been put on a level with the other pews, that perfect gentleman William Sullivan, and his family, used to sit; and, farther down, we heard the resonant voice of Colonel May responding to the minister, as though he were at once Aaron and Hur, ready to uphold his minister, though he did it alone. And there was William Minot, upright and honorable, son of one of Dr. Freeman's dearest friends, whose descendants are with us still; and there were the Curtises, upholders and strengtheners of the society, whose descendants also are with us to-day; and in the broad aisle the Olivers, the Storers, and Bulfinches, and Joseph Coolidge, the first of the line, in the red cloak which, as I remember, was common to gentlemen of that day.

They are all with us here, and with us also those dear friends who have been spoken of with such loyal affection,— Greenwood, who when he came to this Chapel seemed to us who were younger like a very angel of God, charming in person, in voice, in delivery, in gesture, and whose writings also had a charm which will make them remembered as long as English literature remains; and then the dear friend who has been spoken of just now, Ephraim Peabody. Not a word too much has been said of him. He was great in the greatest way; a man of deep but manly piety, without a shadow of pretence of any sort; a man who was independent in the highest degree, and of whose conversation in private I think it may be said that he who heard him talk for half an hour wished to hear him talk on through all the day.

So much must be permitted to one who remembers a great way back; and now, though my friend Wendell Holmes is about to give us a poem, may I venture to read a few lines of verse which I will not call poetry, but which may be a kind of prelude to his opera: —

> As our New England elm, the queen of trees,
> Lifts its vast urn of foliage to the breeze,
> Stirred by each air that thrills its graceful form,
> Or tossing wildly in the driving storm,
> Yet by its mighty roots is anchored fast, —
> So all our life is rooted in the past:
> Through all our struggles, hopes, through good and ill,
> The memories of childhood hold us still.
>
> Church of my boyhood! as we gather here,
> Shades of the past, long buried, reappear.
> I see beside you other forms and faces,
> Another congregation takes your places.
> This dear old church with living lustre burns
> When all the immemorial past returns.
>
> From that old-fashioned pulpit, in my youth,
> Came the calm voice of simple, earnest truth, —
> Words of an honest man, who left the broad
> Highway of custom for a lonely road,
> Firm to resist each rude, opposing shock, —
> Like Hindu temple, cut in solid rock.
>
> And not in vain; for where he made a way
> We enter into Freedom's home to-day.
> He helped to build, with new and better rules,
> Our literature, society, and schools,

WILLIAM DUMMER.
(LIEUT.-GOVERNOR 1716–1730.)

Working with men of every name and creed, —
With Cheverus, though unsainted, saint indeed;
With Mather Byles or Holley took his stand,
Holding a heretic's or bishop's hand;
To all good work his ready help would lend;
Of young and old the counsellor and friend;
And was, when round his form Time's mantle fell,
That "Indian summer" he described so well.

The past is gone! but let the coming race
Keep this old Chapel ever in its place.
Long may it stand for truth, and every son
Join in still better work as time rolls on!
And let its children, wheresoe'er they roam,
Hold fast the lessons of their early home;
And 'mid temptation's wild and stormy blast
May this old anchor ever hold them fast!

THE MINISTER then said: "The Poet who for long years has found a home amid these associations, will now touch for us some of their chords."

POEM.

BY OLIVER WENDELL HOLMES, M.D., L.L.D., D.C.L.

Is it a weanling's weakness for the past
   That in the stormy, rebel-breeding town,
Swept clean of relics by the levelling blast,
Still keeps our gray old Chapel's name of "King's,"
Still to its outworn symbols fondly clings,
   Its unchurched mitres and its empty crown?

Poor, harmless emblems! All has shrunk away
   That made them Gorgons in the patriot's eyes;
The priestly plaything harms us not to-day;

The gilded crown is but a pleasing show,
An Old-World heirloom left from long ago,
   Wreck of the past that memory bids us prize.

Lightly we glance the fresh-cut marbles o'er;
   Those two of earlier date our eyes enthrall:
The proud old Briton's by the western door;
And hers, the lady of colonial days,
Whose virtues live in long-drawn classic phrase, —
   The fair Francisca of the southern wall.

Ay! those were goodly men that Reynolds drew,
   And stately dames our Copley's canvas holds;
To their old church, their royal master, true,
Proud of the claim their valiant sires had earned,
That "gentle blood," not lightly to be spurned,
   Save by the churl ungenerous Nature moulds.

All vanished! It were idle to complain
   That ere the fruits shall come the flowers must fall;
Yet somewhat we have lost amid our gain,
Some rare ideals time may not restore, —
The charm of courtly breeding, seen no more,
   And reverence, dearest ornament of all.

Thus musing, to the western wall I came.
   Departing, — lo! a tablet fresh and fair,
Where glistened many a youth's remembered name
In golden letters on the snow-white stone, —
Young lives these aisles and arches once have known,
   Their country's bleeding altar might not spare.

These died that we might claim a soil unstained
   Save by the blood of heroes; their bequests,
A realm unsevered and a race unchained.
Has purer blood through Norman veins come down
From the rough knights that clutched the Saxon's crown
   Than warmed the pulses in these faithful breasts?

These, too, shall live in history's deathless page,
   High on the slow-wrought pedestals of fame,
Ranged with the heroes of remoter age:
They could not die who left their nation free,
Firm as the rock, unfettered as the sea,
   Its heaven unshadowed by the cloud of shame.

While on the storied past our memory dwells,
   Our grateful tribute shall not be denied, —
The wreath, the cross of rustling immortelles;
And willing hands shall clear each darkening bust,
As year by year sifts down the clinging dust
   On Shirley's beauty and on Vassall's pride.

But for our own, our loved and lost, we bring
   With throbbing hearts and tears that still must flow,
In full-heaped hands, the opening flowers of spring, —
Lilies half blown, and budding roses, red
As their young cheeks before the blood was shed
   That lent their morning bloom its generous glow.

Ah! who shall count a rescued nation's debt,
   Or sum in words our martyrs' silent claims?
Who shall our heroes' dread exchange forget, —
All life, youth, hope, could promise to allure
For all that soul could brave or flesh endure?
   They shaped our future: we but carve their names.

THE MINISTER then said: "The Plummer Professor Emeritus comes to us here as preacher, in a very true sense a pastor long familiar to this church, friend, and fellow-worshipper. No one knows better than he the quality of men who have made this congregation in the past, and the quality that must continue in order to make the Christian church a vital force in the modern world. After him, in closing these services, another will speak to you, in whom many associations meet. A living church cannot live, and will not seek to live, upon its history alone. Together with the backward-looking reverence it will desire to have the forward and the upward look; and so in the name of our memories and our hopes we shall ask Professor Francis Greenwood Peabody to conclude this service."

ADDRESS.

BY REV. ANDREW PRESTON PEABODY, D.D., LL.D.,

Plummer Professor Emeritus in Harvard University.

"THERE shall be like people, like priest." So ran the words of the curse which Hosea pronounced on the house of Israel, — words which, uttered here a century ago, would have been a prophetic benediction, the fulfilment of which we celebrate to-day with gratitude and gladness. But they are less a specific prediction than the statement of a special case under a general law. In all relations, — domestic, social, public, — the tendency to assimilation is inevitable, and in none more truly so than in a Christian congregation. The members of a church choose a minister after their own ideal, which though it can hardly be bad, may be coarse and low; and if they are mistaken in the man, unless they speedily rid themselves of him, they rise or sink toward his level. Conversely, wherever there can be a choice of churches, the minister both attracts and shapes his like; and if he has the best of parishioners, he has borne no small part in making them so. To men and women of even the strongest minds and characters, it is of no little consequence what sort of worship they engage in and what sort of preaching they hear at church. Sunday is the day for receiving, to those who are imparting all the rest of the week. If there be a heart-altar, it depends in large part for fuel on the Sunday pile; and it makes a great difference whether from that pile be fed a mere crackling of thorns, or a steady, generous flame.

The ministers of whose eminent worth you have heard from my brethren could not but have had in their flock men and women of the noblest type, and could not but have made and left their own indelible impress on those to whom they ministered.

My more intimate connection with this church commenced in the autumn of 1860; and its pulpit continued under my charge for more than a year, till the settlement of my very dear friend and pastor, the present minister. During my period of service, the wardens were William Thomas and Gardner Brewer, to both of whom I was indebted for constant and manifold kindness, and whose assiduous care for their sacred charge I hold in reverent memory. It was my privilege to be often with Mr. Thomas during his weary months of decline and suffering, and to see that the principles which had sustained him in an upright and generous life sufficed for his support when all that remained for him was to await the long-lingering summons to go up higher. With him, what a goodly company have passed on to the temple above! And their works have not followed them, but remain for the firmer and higher upbuilding of truth and righteousness. To name only a few of those whom I have known personally, — I recall James Jackson, whose benignant presence fully shared with his surpassing science and skill the conquest of disease and suffering; William Minot, than whom no man ever had more fully the confidence, respect, and reverence of the whole community, who told the secret, the open secret, of his life, when on the margin of the death-river he said, "I have no hope but in my Saviour, — through him alone I have a trembling, yet confident assurance of heavenly happiness;" Charles Pelham Curtis, long a most efficient officer and care-taker of this church, in which he was loved and honored, and but one of a family largely and still identified with the Christian worship, work, and cherished fellowship of King's Chapel; Thomas Bulfinch, by both parents the rich inheritor of ancestral virtues, — an accomplished scholar, too, — whose modesty would have veiled the light of his pure and sweet life, had it not been kindled from that central sun whose rays a meek and lowly spirit cannot hide; John Amory Lowell, toward whom there seemed a perpetual gravitation of trusts of the highest moment, that would have weighed down almost any other man, but which only brought out into the clearer relief his wisdom, his fertility of resource, and his unsurpassed fidelity; Samuel Atkins Eliot, walking in his uprightness in sunshine and in shadow, who could no more have swerved from the right than the stars from their courses; Joseph Coolidge, than whom this church had no more loyal and no more worthy member, his heart-home always here in distant sojourns and in far-off lands; George Barrell Emerson, the pioneer of reformed and truly Christian education, whose school was always a sanctuary, and its training, no less for heaven than for earth; Francis Cabot Lowell, who, in blended dignity and grace, in transparent purity of soul and of life, presented all the traits that go to make up that highest style of man, the Christian gentleman; Edward Pickering, meet representative of a family illustrious equally for public service and for private worth; my friend and classmate, Joshua Thomas Stevenson, who, in the stress of arduous official duty, found time and heart for hardly less arduous work in the Hospital, whose interests, in pure philanthropy, he made his special charge; George Tyler Bigelow, so admirably fitted to preside in a court on whose integrity not a momentary cloud has ever rested. This list which, had I time, I should more than double, I must close with the last of those who have gone from us,— Charles Francis Adams, whose name will gain new lustre with the lapse of years, whom posterity will regard as having borne at least as important a part in our country's second birth as his grandfather in the conflict through which it first struggled into life. These with whom I have worshipped here, and many others of kindred spirit, with not a few saintly women, whom I need not name to recall them to your thought, come back to me from the years that have gone, in living, grateful, loving remembrance.

Such a record craves and claims continuance. These sacred memories ought to be prophetic. My friends of this church, you truly honor its fathers only by being their worthy children. Let what you praise in them not be buried in their graves, but live anew, and ever on, in your loyal Christian life-work. Be it your care to transmit for the next centennial a roll of honor — of the honor that comes not from man, but from God — like that to-day, too full and long to be rehearsed within the memorial hour.

ADDRESS.

BY THE REV. FRANCIS GREENWOOD PEABODY.

Plummer Professor in Harvard University.

IF I were to add anything more than a few brief sentences to what has been already said, I should not only be contributing what was superfluous, but I should soon make some of you suspect that this solemn occasion was to be continued until the two hundredth and two hundred and fiftieth anniversaries were merged into one. Yet there is one note among this series of noble reminiscences which has not yet been struck, and on which one of the younger generation may, for a closing moment, not unfitly dwell. It is the note, not of memory, but of hope. It is the impression not of the backward, but of the forward look. I turn, as we conclude this commemoration, from the past to the future; and I ask, What has this ancient church to say to the new life about it, and to the religion whose forms and methods must change with the changing years? What is the element which this long and honorable history is now ready to transmit as its peculiar contribution to the religion of the future, and which we can now sum up, not alone in terms of reverent reminiscence, but in terms of prophetic hope. I can answer this only as I recall, in perhaps too personal a way, the impression which this church has made upon the one life I happen to know best.

When I look back, as a child of this church, and try to reckon its influence, my first impression is mingled and confusing. Every early experience which I can confess of any sacredness or permanence or depth had its origin and its blessing here. I remember trivial incidents and serious ones, friendships and sermons, festivities and solemnities, the dreams and the prayers of youth; and behind all, there remains the dim reminiscence of one personality of whom I think when I read of the insight given to the pure in heart, and of the life that was founded upon a Rock. Yet when I try to read what lies behind all these different influences, it seems to be plain enough. The fundamental impression made by this church on at least one young life remains entirely distinct. It was not made by its preaching, however eloquent, or by its architecture, however beautiful; but by the subtile atmosphere which has always prevailed here, of reverence, of piety, and of prayer. I thank God that I was born into a church which must be peculiarly described as worshipful. No other impression could be made by a place like this. Surrounded by these monuments of piety, encircled by these graves, set with its repose in the midst of these busy streets, such a place quiets and subdues at its very gateway even the most boisterous boy; nor did I ever know a preacher who could find this pulpit adapted to anything but his most serious, devout, and lofty utterance. I thank God that my first recollections are of this sense of reverence, and that I never can outgrow this view of the function of a church. We hear much about adapting our churches to the life of to-day, and making them social, homelike, and modern. I am thankful that my memories are not of church sociables and parish kitchens, but of a place filled with the sense of God, and in which human associations were subordinated and accessory. We hear much, also, about making the Sunday-school the children's church, and freeing the young from their fatiguing attendance on general worship. I am thankful that I was born before this new *régime*, which puts asunder on the Lord's day the families whom God hath joined together, and which makes the Sunday-school the rival, if not the enemy, of the Church. I owe many debts to faithful teachers here, but most of all am I indebted to them for never creating in my mind any doubt as to where the centre of Sunday lay. It lay for me in the midst of my family in their common worship. It lay for me where I for the most part lay throughout the sermon, —

> "At that best academe, a mother's knee."

I owe more Christian conviction to these circumstances of repose than to all my catechetical instruction; and if there is any blessing which I feel sure is to be permanent for my own children, and which is a blessing for their parents also, it is that they have never yet heard any discussion as to the relative claims of Church and Sunday-school; that church-going is one of their earliest ambitions, and that they are able to find repose in arms which make it a part of worship to welcome and hold them.

I thank God, then, for the influence of a worshipful church; and as I, with the younger generation, look forward from this commemoration of the past to the problems of the future, this is the element of a permanent faith for which we look to a church like this. What the religion of our time has to fear is not that it shall be unscientific in its thought, or unpractical in its conduct. Never before have the churches applied themselves as they are now doing to the worthy tasks of scientific theology and of practical usefulness. But what we have to fear is this: that in this great and wise transition into clearer thinking and better doing we may pass out of the atmosphere of devout feeling and prayerful meditation, the only atmosphere which is religion's native air. We should then be trying to gather the fruits of life without nourishing the roots of life. We should find small gain in the science of religion, if we lost the experience of religion. We should have no legitimate basis for a common life of work, if we had no common life of prayer. Such is the lesson which many a soul has learned, as it has turned alike from its thought and from its work to the influences of this holy place; and such will still be the message of this church to a restless and fretful world. May it still stand among us for the foundations of religion, for reverence, for piety, for worship, so that the young of the new time shall bless it as the fathers of the old time have done! Let the tides of the city ebb with the night about it into rest, and let the returning flood sweep about it with the roar of each new day. Still may it stand, as it so long has done, like a light-house set in the midst of a surging and dangerous sea, with its light kept burning and its message of a quiet harbor for the soul.

After the singing of an Anthem, the services closed with the Benediction by the Rev. JOHN CORDNER, LL.D.

CORRESPONDENCE.

CORRESPONDENCE.[1]

From Official and other Invited Guests.

Mr. OLIVER AMES accepts with pleasure the invitation of King's Chapel to attend the commemorative services on the 15th inst.
BOSTON, Dec. 6, 1886.

MAYOR'S OFFICE, CITY HALL,
BOSTON, Dec. 8, 1886.

DEAR SIR, — His Honor Mayor O'Brien accepts your kind invitation to attend the services at King's Chapel December 15, and thanks the Committee for the same.

Yours respectfully,
N. H. TAYLOR,
Mayor's Secretary.

WAR DEPARTMENT, OFFICE OF THE SECRETARY,
WASHINGTON, Dec. 10, 1886.

GENTLEMEN, — I beg to acknowledge with thanks the receipt of the cordial invitation of King's Chapel, Boston, to attend the services which are to be held on the 15th instant, in commemoration of its completion of two hundred years.

I regret very much that it will not be in my power to be in Boston on that date, and I must therefore forego the pleasure of being present on so interesting an occasion.

I am very truly yours,
WILLIAM C. ENDICOTT.

---

[1] Many letters were received from gentlemen invited to attend the celebration, and a few of them are here given.

SENATE CHAMBER, WASHINGTON, Dec. 8, 1886.

DEAR SIR, — I am very sorry that I cannot attend the services on December 15. The occasion will be one of very great interest to all persons who are proud of the history of Massachusetts; but my duty requires me to be elsewhere on that day.

I am yours very truly,

GEORGE F. HOAR.

---

90 MARLBOROUGH STREET, BOSTON, Dec. 8, 1886.

MY DEAR MR. FOOTE, — I thank you sincerely for your most kind invitation of the 3d instant. It would afford me real pleasure to accept it, and to say a few words at the commemoration of the two hundredth anniversary of the foundation of King's Chapel. But the state of my health at this moment compels me to deny myself to all public occasions.

Though none of the Winthrops of the olden time were connected with your venerable church, I may claim two direct ancestors among those who have a distinguished place in its annals, — Governor Joseph Dudley, and the famous John Nelson. You have mentioned them both in your admirable first volume.

But my own personal associations with your church are far more precious to me. I cannot forget that during not a few of my earlier years I was in the habit of attending afternoon service at King's Chapel, and I can honestly say that I recall the sermons of Dr. Greenwood and Dr. Ephraim Peabody as among the most impressive and inspiring to which I have ever listened. Two more saint-like men I have never known, and their friendship was among the privileges of my life.

I never pass the corner of School Street without rejoicing that King's Chapel has survived the ravages of time and chance, and that it promises to remain as a monument of Old Boston, keeping watch over the graves of the Founders. *Esto perpetua!*

Believe me, dear Mr. Foote, with renewed thanks and warm regard,

Yours very truly,

ROBᵀ C. WINTHROP.

Rev. H. W. FOOTE, Rector of King's Chapel.

THOMAS POWNALL.

(GOVERNOR 1757-1760.)

DORCHESTER, Dec. 16, 1886.

MY DEAR SIR, — I am grateful for your very kind remembrance of me and the card which came so timely as an "open sesame" to the opening services of the third century of King's Chapel, and the closing chapters of the first two. It was not unfitting that old Swansea should have a representation at the gathering, for Samuel Myles, the rector of thirty-nine years from 1689 to 1728, was the son of our John Myles, of Swansea history. Reference is made to Samuel Myles on page 80 of my "Historical Sketches of Barrington." While in the old Chapel I thought also of the grave of an ancestor in the old churchyard, Mary Chilton, of Plymouth Rock tradition.

May I bespeak your kind offices for a copy of the Proceedings of yesterday, when printed?

Most truly,

THOMAS W. BICKNELL.

DORCHESTER, Dec. 12, 1886.

GENTLEMEN, — I am very grateful for the invitation you have extended to me to be present on the celebration of the two hundredth anniversary of King's Chapel. I should enjoy the honor and privilege exceedingly, as I have in my own veins some of the blood which your Rev. Pastor and myself have inherited from the Wilders; but above all to participate with you and the host that will be present on the occasion, in the renown, prosperity, and influence of the institution for the good of our city, and the welfare of mankind. So may it go on prospering and to prosper until we shall have done worshipping in chapels on earth, and finally be assembled in the King's Chapel above.

As ever yours,

MARSHALL P. WILDER.[1]

(1798-1886.)

---

[1] The death of the venerable President of the New England Historic Genealogical Society took place on the day following our services, — December 16, 1886.

From Former Parishioners and Descendants of the Church.

130 Pacific Street,
Brooklyn, N. Y., Dec. 11, 1886.

MY DEAR BROTHER, — It is really very sad for me to be compelled to forego the high satisfaction and pleasure of uniting with you and your people in celebrating the two hundredth anniversary of my ever dear and venerable birthright church. Especially do I value the kind words in which you express the wishes of yourself and of the Committee of Arrangements, that I should be present and offer the Prayer on this most interesting occasion. The latter office thus kindly proffered I deem a marked compliment. Be assured that that prayer is already as fervent at heart as it could be if breathed out in that beloved sanctuary on Wednesday. The condition of my family and a sense of proper regard, at my age and under medical advice, to the risks of the season control me; and thanking you and your Committee most heartily, I yield with as good grace as I can.

But memory will go back to the past, and I must jot down a few of its ramblings. My earliest recollections of the church cluster about the pastor of my childhood and youth, — the venerable, beloved, and saintly Freeman; him who made King's Chapel the pioneer church of our precious and liberal faith in the Republic. That sweet and gentle spirit shone in his every tone and manner, made him delightful in his intercourse with the young of his flock, and his presence in our homes was always an occasion hailed and remembered with pleasure. For his sympathies were the quickest and warmest; he truly rejoiced with them that rejoiced, and wept with them that wept. Never can I forget, when on a Sunday morning my beloved mother — whose image is as fresh as of yesterday in my memory — was lying in the last stage of lingering consumption, and I was about going to church, my father told me to ask Dr. Freeman after service to come home with me. The good man did. My mother was too feeble to speak, but perfectly conscious. Dr. Freeman bent over her to say a few parting words, and then knelt at her bedside in prayer. Her hand lay in his, and the change in his utterance as he prayed, first told us that her angel spirit had fled.

My remembrance of the Doctor's preaching is very distinct from my youth up. His manner was quiet, but earnest and honest, reverent and dignified in its impressiveness. You felt that he meant every word. Yet though prevailingly calm, — far, certainly, from being emotional in public discourse, — so strong and tender were his affections and so keen his sensibilities, that I have seen him in the pulpit so swayed and overpowered by emotion as to be brought to a full stop, unable to utter a word. Notably on one occasion, in preaching a funeral sermon on a dear and distinguished friend, and his audience in full sympathy with him, he was compelled to give way to his tears and sit down.

His style was in general didactic, and his themes largely ethical and practical, addressed to the clear reason and thought of his hearers. But as proof that he could rivet the attention of even the young, I gained when a mere boy my first intelligent impressions of the significance of the early portions of Genesis, and of the Bible itself, from a series of discourses in which he unfolded and justified an allegorical interpretation of the story of Adam and Eve, the Temptation and the Fall. During a college vacation, my attention was so held by two sermons on "The Honest Man," that I begged permission to read and make an abstract of them, — which he at once granted.

As my ordination at Providence, R. I., in 1828 approached, I specially desired that Dr. Freeman should give me the charge. About a year before, on account of bodily infirmities, he had retired from professional duty to his farm at Newton, and I therefore consulted his colleague and successor Dr. Greenwood, who, though feeling confident that he would from necessity decline, thought he would be gratified at being thus remembered, and proposed to go at once with me to Newton. The Doctor received us with his wonted cordiality, and on understanding my errand thanked me ; then, in substance, and in the kindest manner he said : "I wish I could, but it is impossible. I cannot go to Providence. I will charge you, however, here and now." Accordingly, in the most thoughtful and affectionate way, he talked to me on the nature, duties, and responsibilities of the office I was about to undertake. Then, with a spice of humor in his look and manner, — gently whipping my companion over my back, — he charged me to finish my sermons before entering the pulpit, and not (glancing meaningly at his colleague), like some of the brethren, finish them there. He ended by telling us that during the forty-seven years of his pastorate he never worked on his sermons on a Saturday, but kept that day for recreation, visiting, and receiving visits; and on Sunday went fresh to his public duty.

Dr. Freeman's first colleague, as you well know, was the Rev. Samuel Cary. Soon after my mother's death in November, 1813, my father prepared to abandon housekeeping, and Mr. Cary at once proposed that I should live with him till entering Harvard at the next Commencement. This, as it proved, pleasant arrangement took immediate effect. Mr. Cary had no children, and his family consisted of his wife, her unmarried sister, and himself. Excellent and exemplary in all his relations, and thoroughly devoted to his ministry, he proved to me a most kind, scholarly, and Christian friend, helper, and counsellor in my preparation for the University and for maturer life. Happy, most happy was he in his marriage to Miss Atkinson, of Middletown, Conn., a lovely and accomplished woman, in all respects his true help-meet. Together, though childless, their home was all that hearty mutual affection and fidelity, pure and high principle, sincere and unostentatious piety could make it. I have never doubted that its influence, in the ten months during which I shared it, largely determined the early choice and final adoption of my present and long-time profession.

But see still how my fortunes have been associated in some sense all along with King's Chapel, and what reason I have to be thankful for it. After debating the question of a profession some six months after graduation, I at last, to gratify a parent's wish, entered the law-office of one of the noblest members of the Bar and of your parish, the late William Sullivan, — always to the hour of his death a most faithful and endeared friend. No man within my memory has done more honor to the Chapel through his devotedness to its interests, and the purity and elevation of his personal character as a Christian gentleman, than he.

After a long interval I preached two Sundays in March, 1867, in the Chapel; and some half hour before service, on the first Sunday, seated myself in our old family pew (No. 76, broad aisle) to meditate. I was interrupted by the sexton, who saluted me in the easy way of an old acquaintance, and said he had often handed me the wonted foot-stove in my early days. He gave me as his the rare name of Smith, — son and assistant of the sexton of the same name in my boyhood; his successor, and with a son to assist himself. Verily another characteristic illustration of that permanence of things with you to which I am about to allude! I questioned him about the occupants of pews here and there within sight, and to my surprise found them of the same name and lineage with those whose names were familiar in days long gone by. After service I was followed to the vestry room by several gentlemen, and telling the incident, asked your senior warden of that day — the late esteemed William Thomas — how he accounted for this remarkable element of permanence in the Society. He at once replied, "By the use of our Prayer Book;" and the others assented. I was instantly reminded that on my return voyage from Europe, in 1852, I met on the Cunarder the family of a late prominent member of your Society, who I knew had left the New South Church for King's Chapel at the time his friend and pastor at the former — Dr. Greenwood — became minister of the latter. Walking the deck one day with him, I asked if he was reconciled to the use of the Liturgy. He replied: "Entirely. The best proof I can give you is, that preparing for a long absence abroad I put among my luggage copies for each of my family, with three or four extra for friends we might meet; and we very rarely failed, all the time of our absence, to have a Sunday morning service."

It has seemed to me a great privilege, my dear brother, which you are enjoying, and on which I congratulate you, to be the pastor and historian of a church so hallowed by antiquity and sacred by precious memories and an honorable record, — and long may it be your lot! What a cloud of witnesses to its fair fame rise up from the past, as I recall those who filled its pews in my early life! Dalton and Gore and Sullivan and Curtis, — the mural tablets on its walls attesting in stone the worth of the last two, — the Coolidges, May, Bulfinch, Boott, Pratt, Motley, and a crowd of others. Within my knowledge and in my own circle of friendship and fraternity, the Chapel has been too the nursery or primary school of several of our liberal clergy, — Greenwood and Sullivan, and May and Bulfinch, all departed and all honored; and one more who survives, — *primus inter pares*, —

James Freeman Clarke. And "long may he survive" is, I know, your prayer and mine!

Affectionately yours,

FREDERICK A. FARLEY.

FLORENCE, ITALY, Jan. 8, 1887.

MR. FRANCIS C. LOWELL, 50 State Street, Boston:

DEAR SIR, — I have the honor to acknowledge the receipt (yesterday) of the card of invitation from King's Chapel. Please convey to the gentlemen of the Committee my sincere thanks for the most pleasant greeting of the new year, — a token that, after so many years and at such a distance away, I am still remembered in the old stone Chapel. Say to them that I shall never cease to remember the many happy hours during the sixteen years that my voice was lifted in the service of the dear old Church, and that if anything could have drawn me four thousand miles, it would have been once more to join in the harmony on the occasion of her two hundredth anniversary.

Very truly yours,

THOMAS BALL.

Mr. FRANCIS BRINLEY regrets his almost total blindness deprives him of the pleasure to accept the invitation of King's Chapel, to attend the services commemorative of the completion of two hundred years of its existence, especially as two of his ancestors were simultaneously Church Wardens, and that the family tomb is in the cemetery adjacent to the Chapel.

NEWPORT, R. I., December 8.

WORCESTER, Mass., Dec. 4, 1886.

MY DEAR SIR, — Thank you for the kind invitation to attend the services commemorative of the two hundredth anniversary of the foundation of King's Chapel. I accept it with pleasure. Perhaps my college classmate, Rev. Mr. Foote, suggested that an invitation be sent to me because he remembered that my mother was baptized in King's Chapel in 1807. Her father, Samuel Swett, a shipowner, attended church there, living on Winter Street at the time. During my mother's childhood, however, he moved to Dedham; but she often attended services at the Chapel subsequently with her old neighbors on Winter Street and intimate friends, the family of General Dennison, and with her aunt, who had the charge of her after her mother's death, Mrs. Eustis, the wife of General Abram Eustis, whose family while he was in command at Fort Independence attended church at King's Chapel.

Although my mother has just passed her seventy-ninth birthday she feels young, and is still vigorous; and I know that it would gratify her very much to renew the recollections of her childhood and attend the anniversary services to be held on the 15th instant.

Very truly yours,
SAMUEL S. GREEN.

NEWPORT, Dec. 8, 1886.

DEAR SIR, — I thank you most heartily for the invitation to the "commemoration," but I am very sorry that ill health will prevent my accepting it.

Let me not fail, however, to express my interest in King's Chapel. To me it has the most beautiful interior of any church in America. I love to think of it, and "our pew" is distinct far back in childhood. I remember dear old Dr. Freeman. He baptized me seventy-five years ago — almost. Sometimes I have such vivid impression of the baptism — doubtless often told me — that it seems as if I recalled the scene. At any rate I do remember being with other children at the altar, and the catechism and its first question, "Who made you, child?" Pardon this, and with renewed thanks for your attention accept my earnest desires for a happy commemoration, and God's blessing on King's Chapel.

Very truly,
THATCHER THAYER.

From Clergymen.

CLINTON, Dec. 6, 1886.

REVEREND AND DEAR SIR, — Your courteous note has reached me here, inviting me to take part in the very interesting commemoration at King's Chapel on Wednesday next.

Allow me to thank you for the invitation extended to me by the Committee; but official duties in another part of the State will make it impracticable for me to be present.

I am, sir, with much respect,

Yours sincerely,

BENJAMIN H. PADDOCK.

SYRACUSE, N. Y., Dec. 10, 1886.

MY DEAR SIR, — Permit me to acknowledge gratefully the courtesy of an invitation to the approaching historical observance at King's Chapel. I wish my duties here allowed me to be present. My recollections of the months when, a student at Cambridge, I read the service for Dr. Greenwood, are very delightful.

With high esteem, sincerely yours,

F. D. HUNTINGTON.

MEADVILLE, PENN., Dec. 10, 1886.

MR. FRANCIS C. LOWELL:

MY DEAR SIR, — I am heartily grateful to your Committee for the invitation to attend the services commemorating the two hundredth anniversary of King's Chapel, — a place endeared to me by many years' association with its worship and friendship with its minister. Let me wish for the church long endurance, with all its venerable belongings and associations, on the familiar spot; and an even more distinguished service in the future than in the past, for the broad free churchmanship in which it believes, and for which it stands among the churches of our body.

Sincerely and heartily yours,

HENRY H. BARBER.

BOSTON, Dec. 4, 1886.

DEAR MR. LOWELL, — God willing, I shall be glad to be at the King's Chapel commemoration.

Cordially yours,

C. A. BARTOL.

---

626 CARLTON AVENUE,
BROOKLYN, N. Y., Dec. 7, 1886.

MY DEAR SIR, — My thanks are due to your Committee for their kind invitation to the services commemorative of King's Chapel's completion of two hundred years. It will not be possible for me to come, but I congratulate your people heartily upon the long and honorable history of their church; also that this has been so admirably written, and that for a quarter of a century they have had the continuous service of their present minister, and have been glad in him as he has been in them.

Hoping that the anniversary services will be a happy incident of your long career, I am, my dear Sir, and people of King's Chapel,

Very truly yours,

JOHN W. CHADWICK.

NEW YORK, Dec. 14, 1886.

GENTLEMEN, — I should gladly have taken the journey to Boston this evening to attend King's Chapel to-morrow, had I not returned from there last Thursday, and in that visit used up all my time. King's Chapel is venerable to us all for other and better reasons than its fine old age, though that also is a very noble distinction. In my great County of York, in England, there is a grand old monastic ruin, near which some great yew-trees stand, sound and strong, under which men say the masons worked who laid the foundations of the church and home of the brethren.

And the secret of the abiding strength of the great trees, they say, is this, that they cast off what is dead and worthless from the surface, and renew their youth forever at the heart. That is what King's Chapel has done in these centuries, and what its lovers and friends are glad for. If we could all be there, whose hearts beat warm for the shrine which has grown so sacred, the place would not hold us. It *will* hold our good-will and good wishes and warmest greetings; and these I send with all my heart.

Indeed yours,

ROBERT COLLYER,
Minister of the Church of the Messiah.

SHELBYVILLE, ILL., Dec. 11, 1886.

DEAR SIR, — I am sincerely thankful for the invitation to be present at the commemoration of the two hundredth anniversary of King's Chapel. I assure you that but for the long journey required, and pressing engagements at home, I should try to accept the invitation.

I have never been to but one other spot on earth that seemed more hallowed with memories of the past; and that was Plymouth Rock and the Burial Hill of the Pilgrims.

Those early morning prayer-meetings at the Anniversaries of the American Unitarian Association last summer, and the impressive communion service in King's Chapel, seemed to me like a real communion of saints on earth joined with those in heaven. It was a memorable experience to me; and no less was the Sunday following, when I was called to serve in that pulpit. It was a rare experience filled with a strangely sacred awe. How could it be otherwise to one who was born and brought up in southern Illinois, whose mother was born in a fort in this (then) territory over seventy years ago, when the wild Indians were thick, — one whose ancestors came from the Carolinas and Tennessee, and one who, for good reasons, had come to revere the Tri-Mountain city as a sort of Mecca and shrine of sacred memories! Worshipping in that house, I thought of the venerated dust near by, and of the long line of devoted men and women who had spoken and prayed in that house, and whose bodies at last had been tenderly carried from thence to their last resting place.

When I was a lad, about the only book I ever read besides *the* Book was the "Life of Dr. Franklin" written by himself, and I naturally came to regard him then as the greatest man on earth; and to this day a feeling of reverence comes over me when I go near the early haunts of that very wise man, and pass beside the graves of his parents, near King's Chapel. In still later years of my life, the words spoken in the United States Congress that first thrilled me were the words of Charles Sumner; and though I never heard nor saw him in the flesh, I was among those, far away, who wept in sympathy as they read of his funeral service at King's Chapel.

You can see then, how, standing in that dear old Chapel filled with the memories of two hundred years, I was almost overwhelmed with a sense of the presence of those not seen. It was to me a fuller audience room than any in which I had ever spoken. There were no empty seats and no empty space; even the darkest recesses were crowded. It was as if one were walking in a beautiful garden just before the dawn, hearing seraphic music from "the choir invisible," and scenting the fragrance of rare flowers that could not be seen.

Blessings upon the heads of those, — the children of the generations past, — who gather within those walls next Wednesday!

Again thanking you for the kind invitation, and with regret that I cannot be present, believe me, in Christian fellowship,

Yours truly,
J. L. Douthit.

1426 Pine Street, Philadelphia, Dec. 13, 1886.

My dear Sir, — It is with great regret that I have to deny myself the pleasure of being with you on the 15th inst. My eighty-four years are the obstacles. Old age may be hale, as mine is, but it is very brittle.

It is very pleasant, in this changed world, to see in the list of your Wardens and Committee such names as I looked up to with reverence in my youth.

With all good wishes, respectfully,
W. H. Furness.

DOVER, MASS., Dec. 6, 1886.

DEAR SIR, — I thank the Committee for their invitation to the commemoration services of King's Chapel, but shall probably not be in the city on that Wednesday. As one of the many not there who owe something to the brave deed of the Chapel folk *one* century ago, let me send thanks and congratulations to their children.

Yours truly,

W. C. GANNETT.

THE SECOND CHURCH IN BOSTON, FOUNDED IN 1649,
PASTOR'S STUDY, Dec. 6, 1886.

MY DEAR SIR, — With much pleasure I accept the invitation from the Committee to the commemorative exercises of King's Chapel, December 15.

Allow me to take this opportunity to express my cordial fellowship, and that of my church, to the King's Chapel Society and its pastor. The Second Church rejoices in the noble history of its sister church, and congratulates pastor and people on the present vigor and prosperity now existing in it. Both churches have travelled a long way. Our wish for you is the same we express for ourselves, — the age of experience and priceless associations, with renewal of youth and progress.

I am sincerely yours,

EDWARD A. HORTON.

---

176 EUCLID AVENUE, CLEVELAND, Dec. 6, 1886.

MY DEAR SIR, — I write to thank you for the invitation to be present at the King's Chapel commemoration on the 15th inst., and to say that I am really sorry to be prevented by the distance in space between Boston and Cleveland from accepting the same. King's Chapel has borne a very memorable and interesting part in the story of the Unitarian movement in this country, and I would like much to be of the company that will gather to commemorate its service and its long history. Allow me to send

THOMAS HUTCHINSON.
(Governor 1771-1774.)

the sincere congratulations which I may not bring, and to wish for all who may be present a meeting in all ways worthy the signal occasion.

Sincerely yours,

F. L. HOSMER.

---

25 BERWICK PARK, BOSTON, Dec. 8, 1886.

DEAR SIR, — In reply to your kind invitation, permit me to state that it will afford me much pleasure to receive a ticket permitting me to witness the services to be held in commemoration of the completion of the two hundred years of King's Chapel.

Yours very truly,

RAPHAEL LASKER.

MEADVILLE, PA., Dec. 11, 1886.

DEAR SIR, — The polite card received from the Committee of Invitations is most welcome. It reminds me of many things which it is good to remember, both public and private. It tells of the glorious record of your church for two centuries. It has justified its royal name by royal services to Christ and humanity. Liberal and reasonable, it has stood as a bulwark against the fanaticism of free-thinking unbelief. It has demonstrated the value of the Book of Prayer, not only as cultivating the devotional spirit, but as chastening the spirit of individualism and religious freedom, Long may it hold to its sure anchorage in the faith of Christ!

I am reminded too of that dear kinsman of mine, Dr. Ephraim Peabody, whose sweet and hallowed memory is fresh and fragrant as ever, and knows no sere and yellow leaf either in your church or the Unitarian church general.

It would give me the greatest pleasure to be present in body, as I shall be in spirit, with my friend your beloved pastor and the company of the elect on the great day of the two hundredth anniversary of your church; but my duties here will not allow of my absence.

Gratefully and respectfully yours,

A. A. LIVERMORE.

913 Pine Street, Philadelphia, Dec. 7, 1886.

Dear Sir, — I have to acknowledge with great pleasure the receipt of an invitation to attend the two hundredth anniversary of the founding of King's Chapel. I have much doubt whether I can enjoy the peculiar pleasure it would be to me to attend. I most certainly shall come on if next week it should appear possible. I should hardly feel at liberty, there being thus some doubt, to accept a ticket, as they will be in great demand. Yet should I trespass too far if I should say that in case of my not coming it would give me great satisfaction to transfer the ticket to a member of my family (my son) who is in Boston? With your consent I would very gladly avail myself of this alternative privilege.

The Chapel is my ancestral church, as my name will suggest to you; my mother's as well as my father's family having been brought up there, and my parents having been married there. I feel a great desire, if I should not finally be able to come on (which I fear), that our family should not be unrepresented. Please excuse this long note, and believe me

Very truly yours,

Joseph May.

---

219 West 130th Street, New York, Dec. 12, 1886.

My dear Mr. Foote, — I want to thank you for the courtesy of your remembrance upon the occasion of the interesting commemoration services at King's Chapel. At least I presume it is through your kindness the invitation has come to me, for I know no other who would remember me in this connection. I sincerely trust that Wednesday may prove to be all you could wish, and that the patriotic and religious sentiments stirred by the thoughts of days "lang syne" may be a new inspiration to duty to both State and religion.

It is pleasant to remember that I was represented — in my religious ancestry — in the early history of the Chapel, for did not Charles Wesley preach there during his visit to America?

Yours ever,

F. Mason North.

100 MOUNT VERNON STREET, BOSTON, Dec. 11, 1886.

MY DEAR MR. LOWELL, — I am sorry that a service appointed at my church for Wednesday afternoon will prevent my acceptance of the kind invitation of King's Chapel to be present at the service in commemoration on that day.

Allow me to present my congratulations on the two hundredth birthday, and express a wish that the future may become more full than the past of the fruits of the good work for which King's Chapel has been distinguished.

I am yours faithfully,

LEIGHTON PARKS.

---

12 LOUISBURG SQUARE, BOSTON, Dec. 15, 1886.

MY DEAR MR. FOOTE, — In connection with the delightful services at King's Chapel which I have attended this afternoon, I am moved to write you of a little circumstance which brings your church into a brief but pleasant relationship with mine, and which may be new to you. It is that at the formation of our society in 1818, the plate used in the Communion service was obtained from King's Chapel. I quote from an article in Vol. XXXI. of the "New Jerusalem Magazine," written by Henry G. Foster: —

"The Communion was administered at the close of the service, in which, it was said, one or two of the congregation participated who were unknown to us. The plate for the Communion was obtained from King's Chapel by the kindness of the late Col. Joseph May, long a distinguished member of that society."

It is pleasant to me to be able to mention this friendly act, which forms a link, even though it be a slight one, between our two churches.

Fraternally yours,

JAMES REED.

BURLINGTON, VT., Dec. 6, 1886.

MY DEAR MR. FOOTE, — I am much gratified with the invitation to King's Chapel Commemoration, but am obliged, just now, to send to your Committee my thanks, and regrets that I cannot leave home for even that great pleasure and good. You know how glad it would make me to partake your joy. But this must fall under Goethe's and a diviner rule, — "Thou must renounce."

But count me among the reverencers of the Chapel and its honorable years, — among your friends too; also will rejoice with it and you in this happy Festival. May all go well! But it is superfluous to say so. The time itself and the occasion will command their own right success.

Heartily I wish I might be with you, in person as in spirit.

Faithfully,

L. G. WARE.

CINCINNATI, Dec. 9, 1886.

MY DEAR SIR, — I am sorry that distance will keep me from joining in your commemoration of King's Chapel's two hundredth birthday, but I can heartily join in the spirit with the goodly number of people who, whether assembled with you or absent, will rejoice in the noble history of the Church, and in the promise of its long continued usefulness as a centre of religious life and theological progress.

Thanking you for the card of invitation, I am

Very truly yours,

GEORGE A. THAYER.

---

71 CHESTER SQUARE, BOSTON, Dec. 6, 1886.

FRANCIS C. LOWELL, ESQ.:

DEAR SIR, — Accept my grateful acknowledgments for the card of invitation to be present at the commemorative services at the King's Chapel on the completion of two hundred years.

Nothing but necessity will keep me away, and I trust and believe that it may be my good fortune to be with you on that most interesting and memorable occasion.

Dr. Greenwood and Dr. Peabody I knew well, and honored and loved, — gifted and saintly men. George B. Emerson, John A. Lowell, and how many, many more who loved that ancient and hallowed sanctuary — now gone — I was privileged to number as my best and dearest personal friends. Thus that place must ever be to me as the "Gate of Heaven." Long may God's divinest blessing be with you all!

With highest respect,

Most truly yours,

R. C. WATERSTON.

---

243 EAST EIGHTEENTH STREET, NEW YORK, Dec. 12, 1886.

MY DEAR MR. LOWELL, — The invitation to King's Chapel was delayed at my former address, to which it was directed; so please excuse this tardy reply. I am very sorry I cannot be present at the commemoration. It will certainly be a service of unusual interest. I hope some one will explain why the loyal *church-men* who founded the *chapel* should have called it that. Why did they not call it a *church*, — St. Charles's or St. Botolph's, for example? Was it that the foundation was rather political than ecclesiastical? Some of those good founders seem not to have been noted for saintliness. No doubt they were all fine gentlemen, and wore long hair and lace ruffles. But I don't believe the Chapel was ever so Christian an institution as it has been for the last hundred years, and is now. They builded better than they knew.

Yours sincerely,

T. C. WILLIAMS.

BOSTON, Dec. 7, 1886.

DEAR SIR, — It will give me pleasure to attend the services in commemoration of the two hundred years during which King's Chapel has shed light upon men.

With cordial thanks for the invitation,

I am, respectfully,

WM. BURNET WRIGHT.

CONCORD, MASS., Dec. 16, 1886.

MY DEAR MR. FOOTE, — I want to congratulate you and your beloved church on the great success of your two hundredth anniversary celebration yesterday. It was, indeed, a memorable occasion, and one that must have made you and your good people feel that you were richly repaid for all the labor and care which it cost you. The services at the very outset were pitched to a high key, nor lost for a single moment on to the end their wonderful interest, earnestness, dignity, and Christian spirit and power. What other American church could gather about itself such a wealth of historic associations, or bear a better or more beautiful testimony to a continued fidelity to the truth that is in Jesus and the faith that is unto salvation? The Unitarianism for which King's Chapel has so long and so consistently stood, which found such noble and eloquent expression in the many varied yet accordant voices of yesterday, and what called forth the well-merited and magnificent tribute that was paid by the famous and honored rector of Trinity, — is there any form of religion which is at once more reasonable, Scriptural, comforting, and inspiring than that? Thank God for it, and for the church that with its successive ministers has been so loyal to it, and has so signally and finely exemplified and illustrated its grace and truth!

What has thus recently been said and done, in connection with your bi-centennial commemoration, will have a powerful effect to make many souls more believing and devout, and to confirm them in their allegiance and love to the common Master.

And so, dear brother, I give you joy, and am most glad that your lot is cast in such pleasant places, and that you are so worthily perpetuating the sacred tradition and Christian usefulness of the church of your affections; and with warmest regards and all best wishes for you and yours, I am, as you know,

Ever fraternally and faithfully yours,
A. P. PUTNAM.

CLOSING SERMON

BY

Rev. HENRY WILDER FOOTE,

PREACHED IN

King's Chapel, Boston,

Dec. 19, 1886.

SERMON.

Our holy and our beautiful house, where our fathers praised thee. — *Psalms* LXIV. 11.
That he might present it to himself a glorious church, not having spot or wrinkle, or any such thing; but that it should be holy and without blemish. — *Ephesians* v. 27.

THE pictures of the outer and of the inner Temple are here set before us, — that of a sanctuary venerable, beloved, and sacred by long association and holy use; and that of the spiritual building for the sake of which all this exists, — to build up a community of souls, each in itself and all together in holiness and righteousness.

These are the blended thoughts which seem to belong here to-day, when we stand freshly among the memories which have been so revived for us, and ask ourselves what is the great impulse which we should take forward into this new century of our parish life for our inspiration. For there are certain things very definite, very positive, and very helpful, which come to us to make us feel that we stand not so much at the end of a great history, but at the beginning of a work which we can do in worthy continuation and even larger increase of that which has been so rich and full and fruitful in the long past.

We must feel indeed to-day, as never before we have felt it as a church, how living the past is, how wealthy in teaching and in inspiration.

It is largely due to the forward-reaching and eager temper of our time that an influential school of modern thinkers has been led to adopt, as one of the cardinal principles of their philosophy, the axiom that it is of little value to study the records of the past at all. The world starts fresh with each new generation, it is said. What would be the advantage in a man's going back to his own cradle in order to learn how to take care of himself, or returning to his first school in order to learn how to manage his business? The history of the past is the record of quarrels that fought themselves out and had better be forgotten, or of dreams that have faded into thin air, or of ideas, crude and partial, that have been outgrown by the world's advance. Study real facts, it is said, — the solid things that are always true, and once found out will remain the same forever. Leave the childhood of the world to take care of itself, and take the knowledge which is round you on every side.

Now, I am far from disparaging the importance of the solid facts which these thinkers exalt to exclusive worth. By all means let the measuring rod and the balances weigh and measure the whole of the visible creation; let the laws which bind the universe together be deciphered, and the human mind still "go sounding on its dim and perilous way." But still, when we speak of solid facts, is anything in the constitution of the earth or of the elements of the sun more substantial than the things which men have lived? Shall the fossil slab on which extinct creatures have left their footprints, or the petrified mud-beach which has been pelted by drops of rain in some remote epoch, be more significant to us than the monument of some far-off achievement of human courage or human faith, or than some immortal page which glows with the narrative by a soul of genius of deeds which shed lustre on the human race? But, it is said, humanity is progressive, and the law of progress bids us look forward and not back. It seems to me that this mode of thought (and it is one which has colored many of our minds, even though we do not sympathize with the general drift of the school of thinkers who propound it) is really a confusion of thought arising from a mistaken carrying out of the analogy of progress. Because in the progress of a ship through the sea the waters close again behind it; because in that of a man through the street the whole of him goes forward, — it is imagined that the race in like manner, when it advances, takes the whole of itself with it. Whereas the fact really is, that human progress means the addition of resources, knowledges, and faiths to the accumulated store which it already possesses, and not the perpetual substitution of new for old. That people is the richest people which adds its present gains to the largest fund, so to speak, of heroic memories and wise experiences and deeply impressed lessons from older time.

But we need only appeal to our own experience. We find every day that we do not cut our lives in twain, and put out of sight and out of thought all our own past. We live on its accumulated capital of principles of action, rules of conduct, moral convictions, religious assurances, which have accrued to us bit by bit out of the slow years ever since we began to think at all. We look back in order to go forward, — just as it is the backward-stretching foot which gives the impulse, as we walk, which sends us on. Is it less so in the advance of humanity? Can we hold for a moment that the present, so long as it is *present*, is to be all-absorbing, and the moment it is past is to be utterly worthless; that it is valuable to us while it is filled with dust and turmoil and pettiness, but good for nothing when the cloud which darkened it while shaken sinks to the bottom and leaves its eternal truths clear?

Indeed, it is hardly necessary for us to reason with ourselves on this point; for all our reasonings will not weigh so much with us as those spontaneous instincts which rise up on special occasions and recall us to a sense which after all is deeper than our theories, — that the treasure of great public memories is a mighty heritage, in which history is full of the most present influence over our lives.

PETER FANEUIL.

(1700–1743.)

And we see at once why such a past, as has just been held up before us in the illuminating testimony of many witnesses, should be one of God's most potent ministers of teaching for us. It has one precious use which the present cannot have, from the very fact that it is more remote from us. We cannot always look dispassionately, if we would, at the great questions which are bound up with the application of religion to our own case. The very strength of our need of these helps and powers affects us too deeply to let us always feel sure that we can trust even the spiritual instincts which mightily affirm the truth of what the Christian Church offers in its Master's name. But when we study the working out of this religion by men remote enough from us to be unobscured by the mists of our own mental and spiritual atmosphere, we are taught to believe in its enduring and supreme value. You have seen how wonderfully mere distance and elevation map out for a traveller the way by which he has journeyed. He goes on by a dusty road, seeing only a little way before or behind, but climbing, climbing, as the way winds, till at last he stands on the highest ridge of the line of hills that has enclosed his forward vision; from that fresh, cool height he looks back to find the whole way that he has travelled laid out before him. What was blind before is now clear. Not only the way that he has come, but the whole surrounding landscape and the way which lies before him stand forth.

It is so with the journey which our parish has been taking from the earliest beginning of its history. In the present, we can hardly see much more than the present; but when we look back we see not only the past, we really see the present too,— how this came out from that, and what this really is. It has well been said, "The history of our race is experience without the drawback of passion." The experience of these two hundred years as we look back upon it, even in the partial glimpses which are all that the mysterious privacy of each human soul with its God allows to us, is the heaped up testimony of a multitude of God's children to the moral order and spiritual truth which govern the world. We see the history acted out by conspicuous persons in a great arena, and we are tempted to linger on what may be called the drapery and costume of the actors; but we fail to look with the spiritual sympathy which alone can understand the real motive of their deepest lives, until we touch in them a human nature like our own, working out the great problems of destiny and duty under the light of the gospel of Jesus Christ, and with the aid of his Church. In some we behold clearly manifest how religion has softened and mellowed the rugged nature, in others the springs of gentler and nobler spirits are visited by the reviving grace of God; but I do not see how any one can consider the fact which the living on of a church through seven generations indicates, without being profoundly impressed by its accumulated witness to the reality of the help and blessing for which the Church stands.

I try to picture to myself those successive generations of worshippers here as they come and go, while the church remains. They are very distinct each from each, and all from our modern world in which every one is blended in an indistinguishable mass, and the monotony of dress seems to indicate a similar monotony of color and expression in mind and soul.

First pass by the earliest group of the founders, on whom we dwelt in former discourses. They seem like persons who have stepped out from Lely's or Kneller's canvases, as they bring here not the dress only, but the manner and carriage of the Stuart court, — the armor and brilliant attire, the step and look and haughty bearing of those who represent the loyalty to kings reigning by divine right, among a people who have already breathed this free air for two generations. Let us speak their names once more — those of Andros and his lady, of Nicholson and Nelson, of Randolph and the worthy rector Ratcliffe — before they vanish from us into the remoter past as we enter our third century.

Those of the next generation are harder to distinguish, yet not a few names survive to us — Foxcroft and Lyde, Dyer and Newton, Southack and Jekyll — of those who are somewhat more than names, as they listen during the long ministry of Rev. Samuel Myles, and of the King's lecturers, Bridge and Harris. We hear the noise of successive controversies within and without the church. It is a time of quarrel in Church and State. The days of good Queen Anne and of the First George pass before us, and the rougher as well as the gentler touches depicted in Sir Roger de Coverley.

Another generation presses on the former. They come from stately homes set deep in gardens on streets at the North End of the town, or from Cambridge and Medford mansions, enriched from West India plantations and waited on by black slaves, — the Vassalls and Royalls, Mascarenes and Brinleys, Gibbins and Read, Auchmuty and Faneuil; Sir Harry Frankland, the gay young Collector of the Port; and Rector Price, commissioned by Bishop Gibson as his commissary for New England, drawn by the attractions of his country home and mission at Hopkinton more and more away from the town.

So it is that we come at last to the laying of the corner-stone of this new church in 1749. Governor Shirley, waited on by Mr. Caner in his prime, and the wardens and vestry stand round the slab inscribed "Quod felix faustumque sit Reipublicae," then go into the old church still enclosed in the trench for the new foundations, and hear the sermon on "The Piety of Erecting Churches to the Honour of God." Let those second founders of the church, to whom we owe this sanctuary which has been a home to so many for more than one hundred and thirty years, pass before us a moment, — the Governor, nobly urging forward the design of building

when all others were discouraged, saying that it was
"not for themselves, but posterity," and encouraging
others by a lavish subscription; Charles Apthorp,
"the greatest merchant on this continent," whose
descendants still worship among us, treasurer and
chief mover in the building; Barlow Trecothick,
later Lord Mayor of London; Dr. Sylvester Gardiner, lord of a great domain to the eastward; Cradock and Hawding and Paxton.

Yet another group now hurries by, in which some
of those whom I have just named, now growing old,
are the leaders, — Deblois and Erving, Price and
Hutchinson, Chardon and Johonnot, Vincent and
Brimmer. The church suffers with the darkening
times. It is built, but not yet fully paid for, and
the grass-grown streets of the turbulent town yield
little revenue to its members. Still they pray loyally
for King George, "that he may have the victory over
all his enemies," till that March Sunday comes which
sees them kneeling here for the last time. The old
rector gives the benediction, and they go out of
these doors like Adam and Eve from Paradise, with
backward, tearful look, that would be sadder yet if
they fully knew how the angel with flaming sword
would stand at the portal to prevent their return.

The fifth generation now appears within these
pews, around the youthful reader Freeman, as he
urges the changes in the liturgy, and once more the
sound of discussion is heard, — Dr. Bulfinch and the
younger Gardiner, Joseph May and Ebenezer Oliver,
Minot and Amory, Templeman and Coolidge among

those who favor, Ivers and Dehon and Haskins among those who oppose, alteration.

And now we are in this present century, beginning with such men as I have just named, — among them all Joseph May, perhaps the most serviceable to the church during more than fifty years' connection with it, — and ending with the goodly company of those of whom some names were mentioned here on Wednesday with fit honor, as types of many more like them.

It is far easier to trace the outward history of this church during most of its two hundred years, especially in its great historical and picturesque aspects, than to trace its inward and spiritual history. This is always so, indeed; especially where, as in our case, the martial music of England, the triumphs of great deeds of war, the thunders of the Revolution are almost constantly in our ears during the first half of this long time; and during both the earlier and the later days the long roll of worshippers here is constantly lighted up by the names of men round whom the history of their time revolved, or who, if less widely known, were building up this community in its best undertakings and character. The names of some of them, from the long succession of royal governors whose escutcheons hang here again to-day as they did a century and a half ago, to some of those worthy and good of our own day, were lately spoken again in your hearing. Of others, a long procession, time failed us, and is now wanting, to speak; yet it is well to remind ourselves that in all this long period few persons of note have visited Boston who have not entered here. I like to think that Washington was in this church once and again, — when he came a survivor of Braddock's rout, to tell Governor Shirley of his son's death in that disaster, and sat, a young man in his Virginia colonel's uniform, in the Governor's pew; and again as first President of the United States, — while these walls are the only building remaining unchanged in Boston which saw the entry of his besieging army midway between those two points of time. It is pleasant to hear it recalled in what pew the mighty brow of Daniel Webster used to be seen, when from time to time he appeared in this company of worshippers; and that the elder and the younger President Adams are remembered here, as well as their illustrious descendant who has so recently passed to their companionship.

But let us not be dazzled by the old splendors of courtly pageants and great public events and high personages, which echo or are seen here the moment we stop long enough to listen to the voice of the great past, — so as to forget that all the time a real spiritual history has been evolving itself in many souls through seven generations. It has well been said: "But while we recall from the past the outward history of this church, we cannot help remembering that within it all there ran a deep spiritual history that developed into richer and more enduring forms than architectural products. What chapters of religious biography were frescoed upon the walls of those old churches, not visible to human eyes, but seen by God and the ministering angels! How many understandings were divinely taught, and stricken hearts healed, and longing souls filled, and wavering wills confirmed for God! . . . It must have been so. God would not let his Gospel live an unfertile life so long. The covenanted presence went with the holy things of the temple, and Christ was in the midst of his disciples according to his word."

We are not left to imagination in trying to represent to ourselves what was the spiritual food on which those earlier generations were fed here. They belonged to the Church of England in its eighteenth-century form, and shared its thoughts, and doubtless were shut in by its limitations. The library which King William III. gave to the King's Chapel, and which is preserved, shows what books our earlier ministers read and doubtless distilled into many a sermon. The divine rights of rulers and the apostolic claims of the Church must have made a part of the teaching of the church which stood here confronted with the children of Puritanism. The doctrines of Orthodoxy were taught, but in a somewhat gentler form than that proclaimed in their churches. The imagination of Jeremy Taylor must have lighted up some of the sermons preached here; but they were probably built for the most part on the lines laid down by Tillotson, Beveridge, Sherlock, and Butler, — the clear, calm, cool method of converting by argument from the evidences of Christianity, and appealing to a utilitarian philosophy to make men good for their best advantage in both worlds. Such is the groundwork of those few discourses by our earlier ministers, — Myles, Harward, Price, and Caner, — which have survived to us. Meantime, however, we know that mightier voices were heard here or in the wooden church, chief among them that of Charles Wesley, — the father, in a better sense than even his brother John, of that great spiritual renewal of English life which we call Methodism. Here, too, Bishop Berkeley preached, — the author of a system of pure idealism in philosophy as against the common-sense philosophy of the school of Locke. And George Whitefield, the mightiest preacher whose tones ever shook the sinner's soul, here sat a silent worshipper only, and had to seek his audiences in Dissenting meeting-houses or on the Common.

The type of religious character which the churches of that century educated was marked with the defects as well as the strengths of the time. It did not believe in fervors. "Enthusiasm" was its special dread. Yet side by side with its quiet training of the sober virtues of character and of religious habits, we can trace in the letters and diaries of men and women who worshipped here in those old days a devout dependence upon God and sense of communion with him, which show how genuine and vital was the living faith which was nourished here by the prayers and the altar which were the heart of the church.

With the later period we come into a time which is known to us more directly, either by memory of more recent years or by tradition. Still, the general habit of this parish remained. The changes in its liturgy did not violently sunder it, in its own feeling, from the past, however they might seem to others. What they did was to relieve the consciences of the worshippers by omitting that which seemed to them not Scriptural, and bringing the worship into accord with the language of the Bible, which to all Christians is the most hallowed of books. Nor did the character of the preaching change as much as might be supposed. Dr. Freeman's mind was also shaped by the eighteenth-century divines. His philosophy was that of Priestley. On disputed doctrine he hardly ever preached, after the few sermons a hundred years ago which led his people to modify the prayer-book. His sermons were practical, unemotional, devoted to edifying his people in practical goodness and charity. A warmer glow of feeling and a deeper spiritual insight enriched this pulpit under his successors, to whom you heard such testimonials at our service of commemoration. But throughout, as I read the history of this parish, its solid, sober, genuine religious qualities remained the same. We know what the character, not moral only but religious, has been, the sturdy strength and pillared rectitude, which has made men sure what they could find here, and made this church stand for something like its own house of worship in this community, — as King's Chapel itself stands in these streets with firm, solid, rocky walls, but within, perhaps unknown by the multitudes who pass and repass, a very shrine of faith. We know, too, many of us, the hidden things of religious experience in which souls have found here, and still find, that God is not far from them, and the call of Christ rouses all within them to "rise up and follow."

The immense changes which have altered all the habits of life more in the last fifty years than in the previous five hundred introduce new and difficult problems in regard to the Church, and especially, perhaps, in regard to such a church as this. No thoughtful person can avoid seeing or can help regretting the loosening of the bonds of religious habit in great communities like our city. The causes for it are many, — some of them are bad, some not wholly so, or are at any rate, in the particular case of the men and women who have dropped the church-going habit out of their lives, the natural result of a whole network of conditions in which they are bound. It by no means follows, indeed, that because they can hardly help it they are not hurt by it. Nor because the American Sunday is not yet shaped into its final form, does it by any means follow that it will end by being no Sunday at all, or that the Church and the great institution of public worship are going to fade away under our Western sky. Still, the case is very different with any particular church in the loosely knit multitude of heterogeneous and often indifferent persons that make up the mass of a large city, from what it was in the compact town of our fathers, where everybody went to church, talked about it, and often, it must be confessed, fought about it.

Two special difficulties confront this church, the necessary result of the growth of Boston; and both have come in our own time. When this house was built, it stood near the westward limit of population. The great hill which rose with its beacon just beyond, like a wall held back the tide upon this side; and the church sat as a queen among the happy homes of its people that nestled in the crooked lanes and streets of the old town. Probably there was hardly a house in the parish so far away as not to hear the deep note of our bell calling to worship, in the profound hush and Sunday quiet of the town. Only those dignitaries who came in state in their chariots from the suburbs, by the roundabout way across the Neck, or crossing the Ferry from the northward, were beyond its reach. But now for a quarter of a century the sun as it moves toward its setting has steadily been drawing the habitations of this people after it, as the moon draws the tides; and while other churches have floated with the current, this is anchored fast in its old holding-ground. True, its hold upon the affections and loyalty of its members is exceptionally strong. Our commemoration must have made us all feel that, and feel why it is so. But the cable is continually lengthening by which they are held to it.

REV. JAMES FREEMAN.

(READER 1782; RECTOR 1787–1836.)

And then there is the enormous change which has come over all the fixed family life of the old time, in consequence of the altered summer habits of our community. In the old time, the only home was within almost a stone's throw of this spot; and on all the fifty-two Sundays of the year the preacher knew that he would see the bulk of his congregation in their familiar places. But now, perhaps you do not even yourselves quite know how universally it is otherwise. I believe that members of this parish have permanent summer homes of their own in at least sixty different New England towns and villages, besides the wider migration which every season brings. For several months of every year, I can count on my fingers all the families who remain at home in the city, and for a still longer time this church has vast desert spaces intervening between its inhabited spots. Even those of you who go only to a short distance have church relations for a considerable part of the year there and not here, and the country churches rightly depend on the help which thus comes within their doors.

Thus the conditions are altered in two respects: 1. As regards the work of the church itself, it becomes more and more clear that during that portion of the year it should set its face steadily to do what it can for the multitudes that never cease to pass here winter and summer. When its proper work as a parish family church shrinks like a brook in its channel under the midsummer sun, it has still a gospel to preach and a work to do, and those who are absent from it should know that this work is still being done. 2. As regards the members of this parish, I would ask you to feel that the modern freedoms and enlargements of your life do not emancipate from the duty of standing by and showing your belief in your church. If the time when it can do its full work and show itself in complete life and strength is shortened to six or seven of the twelve months, all the more does your church ask you not to let any light thing stand between you and it, when you are within reach of it. If we have to compress our life into a fraction of the year, all the more let us be really alive in that. And then there is much in keeping faithful the loyal habit of thinking of your church when you are absent from it. We can carry it with us to a peculiar degree. This Book of Prayer which contains so much of its worship and its character is ready to bring the atmosphere of its devotions and the very shadow of its pillared arches into your summer Sundays, and to keep you in accord with the deep thoughts which belong here. I am glad to testify that not a few do so feed the springs of their own souls while absent from this old home of their faith, — as I have seen in the far West the waters led down from the snowy heights of the Wasatch Mountains to irrigate the thirsty plains below fainting under the hot sun, and flowing freshly through dry and dusty places, to make "the wilderness blossom as the rose;" and then when the stream of life flows back here again it fills our fountains full of life and power.

Moreover, in the wide changes which have come over the churches of various names, a Christian church, with the double and blended inheritance which is peculiarly ours, has a large work to do, if it will loyally and faithfully set itself to the full use of its opportunities. It occupies a mediatorial position, so to speak, in relation to widely divergent states of thought and feeling in this age of fluent and fermenting opinions. Few of us have an adequate sense of the modification of thought, still more of the enlargement of charity, which is going on in what are called the Orthodox bodies around us. There can be no doubt that many in the Trinitarian Congregational Church of New England to-day regret the spirit and policy which prevailed in that body seventy years ago, and which excluded the Unitarian Congregationalists from that communion. In the Protestant Episcopal Church a spirit broad, noble, and generous is resolutely striving against a more narrow, hard, and arrogant temper. The great problem which American Christendom has to solve is the question how to reconcile a wise conservatism with a rational spirit of progress. Toward that solution it seems to me that a church can do something — perhaps much — which occupies historically and religiously the mediatorial ground where this church has been placed by the providence of God. I am fain to think that something has been done to bring the kingdom of God nearer by the welcome and respectful hearing which has been given here in recent years to men like the beloved Diman, too early taken from us, and to others of the same generous Christian sympathies among the living. Whoever represents in the different branches of the Church of Christ the spirit of light, of truth, of faith, which alone can lift American Christendom out of mere sectarianism into a higher and serener air, ought to be at home in a church which seeks to shape its worship and its faith according to the New Testament of our Lord and Saviour Jesus Christ.

In this transitional time the peculiar denominational freedom of King's Chapel ought to be very precious to us. By the course of events in the past, this church was compelled largely to stand alone. It has never since so entered into other ecclesiastical relations as to subject itself to the vote or authority of any other organization. To-day, in fraternal good-will to all, and especially to those most in affinity with our profound conviction that Jesus Christ is larger than any men's interpretations of him, it will sympathize with those things which make for the cause of that simple, broad, unsectarian yet positive Christianity which is in the line of its traditions and its worship and its faith. Whatever is discordant therewith it will frankly dissent from; and never, so long as it is faithful to its religious history and to the reverent Scriptural usages of its Christian tradition, can it give aid or sympathy to anything which is not supremely loyal to its Master and Lord.

The question of methods and details of parish

work hardly belongs in this larger survey which we have been taking of our whole position and opportunity. Yet we must not forget that it is the duty of those who love their church to be ready to learn from the new time whatever it has to teach in these ways. There is not a little in the modern machinery of church life which does not really help the true life of any church; and there are things, too, which are suited for one church but not for another. But it would be strange if in two hundred years nothing had been discovered of universal value in religious administration. I believe that if this parish will look for such helps and use them, its later centuries may be its best as well as its most useful. In these later years some such steps have been taken, greatly, as we all agree, for the common good and life. Other things have been proposed, but have not commanded that general agreement which is vital to success; yet they still appear to me, in looking to the future, to be wise and necessary for the adequate enlargement of the parish life and work.

This parish has had the gift of stability to an unusual degree, not only standing on the same spot for seven generations, but standing solidly in the same general characteristic qualities, and even continuing the tradition of family parish life through all. We still have with us descendants of a subscriber to the first building, two hundred years ago, and not a few representatives of those who built this statelier church, and many who are here in the third and fourth generation. Many, too, are with us who have come in these later days, and take their honored part no less with us. It is in this blending of the old with the new, of the new with the old, that not a little of our strength consists. It is for the children of this generation to continue that sense of belonging here, of caring for their church and intending to serve it, if it is to go on with the life of the new century as it went with those before. I would plead especially with the men of this parish to remember how much depends on their interest and care and faithfulness, for the help or the hurt of the best life of their church.

As we look back on the long story, there are reasons why we may well recall it, not as an antiquarian record, nor even only as a great chapter of history, full of light and color, to take pride in. It is good for us to dwell upon, till we feel ourselves also a part of the procession of the generations; for it makes on us a constant impression of character, of religion, and of stability in the best things. Those men who really give the parish its life, as far back as we can see them through the mists of the past and down to those who made it a quarter of a century ago, are essentially the same in solid worth, in self-reliant sturdy vigor, compelling in each age the respect if not always winning the liking of the world around, — men willing to contend for their convictions and (what is much harder) to suffer for them. These men have stood for something substantial and sure, and their church has so stood, all the way along.

We trace the thread again, from the old loyalty and the old history, through the inspiring witness of this church, through its best lives, to the glory of the Christian ministry and the largeness of the Christian work of a living church, — its memories which inspire rather than sadden; its great teaching of worship and reverence; its conserving of the moral and spiritual treasures which the ages have so painfully won and may so easily misprize. But the Church should be something more than a conserver; it should also be an inspirer. These treasures are ours to keep, not by hiding in a napkin, but as the woman in the parable hid the leaven in three measures of meal till the whole was leavened; or as the children of Israel had the sacred ark of the covenant, not to sit down beside it as something too holy to move, but that it might march before them in the wilderness. So the story of what this church has done would not be complete unless you could tell not only that it had guarded well the accumulated sacredness of what prophets saw and apostles proclaimed, of what the slow experience of the believing generations has assured to us, but that here constantly new souls had been fired with the vision of God's truth, lifted above their weakness by His strength, out of their temptations and darkness into His light, — the Living Witness of the Spirit making the old new by the present power of the Christ of God.

And now, as we stand at the beginning of this new century of our church life, may it be with new hope and fresh courage for the untried way that opens before us, — resolved that we will look for God to lead us to larger vision, and that we will rise with His help to our opportunity, holding fast to all that He has given us, pressing forward ever to " that which is before."

INDEX.

1

INDEX.

AARON and Hur, 129.
Adams, Charles Francis, tribute to, 137.
Adams, President, 177.
Addington, Mr., 27.
Ainsworth, Henry, psalmody of, 18.
Allen, Rev. John, 46.
American process, the, 23.
Ames, Lieut.-Gov. Oliver, 73; letter from, 145.
Amory, John, 175.
Andrew, Gov. John A., brings bodies of Massachusetts soldiers to King's Chapel, 87.
Andros, Lady, 83, 173.
Andros, Sir Edmund, description of, 24, 26, 42, 44, 45, 46, 63, 83, 91, 173; commission of, 43; arms of, 62; portrait of, 71; founder of the earliest church, 100.
Anne, Queen, 63, 174.
Antego, 40.
Apthorp, Charles, 85, 175.
"Arbella," the, 35.
Atkinson, Miss, 150.
Auchmuty, Robert, 174.

BALL, Thomas, letter from, 152.
Bankes, Richard, 64.
Baptists, the early, 20.
Barber, Prof. Henry H., letter from, 154.
Bartlett, J. C., 66.
Bartol, Cyrus A., D.D., letter from, 155.
Bay Psalm Book, The, 31.
Beacon Hill, 31.
Belcher, Gov. Jonathan, 63; arms of, 62; portrait of, 70.

Bellomont, arms of the Earl of, 62.
Berkeley, George, Bishop of Cloyne, 179.
Bernard, Sir Francis, 63.
Berry, J. K., 66.
Beveridge, William, Bishop of St. Asaph, 178.
Bicknell, Thomas W., letter from, 147.
Bigelow, Hon. George Tyler, tribute to, 137.
Bishop of London, Randolph's letters to, 21, 24, 25.
Blackburn, Jonathan B., artist, 84.
Blake, Mrs. George Baty, 74.
Boott, the family of, 151.
Bossuet's varieties of Protestantism, 20.
Boston, evacuation of, 63, 65.
Boys and negroes in the early congregation, 24.
Braddock's rout, 177.
Bremen, the Rathhaus of, 35.
Brewer, Gardner, 135.
Bridge, Rev. Christopher, 64, 85, 173.
Brimmer, Martin, 175.
Brinley, Francis, letter from, 152.
Brinley, the family of, 174.
British Army and Navy, officers of, 84.
Broad Street, the, 31.
Brockwell, Rev. Charles, 64.
Brooks, Phillips, D.D., 60; address of, 112.
Buckminster, Rev. Joseph Stevens, 128.
Bulfinch, Rev. Stephen Greenleaf, 151.
Bulfinch, Dr. Thomas, 175.
Bulfinch, Thomas, tribute to, 136.

INDEX.

Bulfinch, the family of, 129, 151.
Bulfinch, Madam, gift of, 65.
Bullard, Francis, 66.
Bullivant, Benjamin, 64.
Bunker Hill, 63, 86.
Burnet, Gov. William, 63; arms of, 62; portrait of, 70.
Burnett, Deacon John, gift of, 65.
Butler, Joseph, Bishop of Durham, 178.
Byles, Rev. Mather, 131.

CANER, Henry, D.D., 64, 84, 95, 179; sermon on laying corner-stone of King's Chapel, quoted, 88.
Canterbury, William Sancroft, Archbishop of, 38.
Cary, Nathaniel, gift of, 65.
Cary, Rev. Samuel, 64, 74; tribute to, 150.
Catechising of children in King's Chapel, 153.
Chadwick, Rev. John W., letter from, 155.
Channing, William Ellery, D.D., 128.
Chardon, Peter, 175.
Charles the First, King, 14, 19, 22; beheading of, 48, 49.
Charles the Second, King, 19, 22, 25, 49.
Charles River, the, 37.
Checkley family, arms of the, 62.
Cheverus, Jean Louis Anne Madeleine Lefevre de, Bishop of Boston, 131.
Christ Church, Boston, services in, 34, 85.
Christ Church in Philadelphia, 102.
Church and State, seventeenth-century idea of, 47.
Church of England, feared by the Puritans, 21; first meeting of members of, 38; first administration of the prayers and ordinances of, 63; worship of the, first had by authority, 82; parishes in Boston, 85.
Clark, one Mr., 40.
Clarke, James Freeman, D.D. 4, 61, 127, 152; address of, 128; poem by, 130.

Clarke, Rev. Josiah, 64.
Clarke, Miss Sarah H., 70.
Collects read in Commemoration Services, 77, 78.
Collyer, Rev. Robert, letter from, 155.
Commemorative Services, description of, 69; programme of, 53–66.
Committee, report of plan of celebration of 200th Anniversary, 4.
Common Prayer, first public administration of, 28.
Commonwealth, portrait loaned by the, 62.
Communion plate of King's Chapel, 65, 78, 85.
Compton, Henry, Bishop of London, 44.
Congregational Churches, watch and ward of, 22.
Consecration service for a church, quoted, 80.
Coolidge, the family of, 151.
Coolidge, Mrs. Catharine, gift of, 65.
Coolidge, John G., 66.
Coolidge, Joseph, 129, 175.
Coolidge, Joseph, tribute to, 137.
Coolidge, J. Randolph, jr., 3, 6, 53, 64.
Coolidge, J. Templeman, 3d, 6, 53; services of, 72.
Copley, John Singleton, 132.
Cordner, Rev. John, LL.D., 61.
Correspondence on the occasion of the 200th Anniversary of King's Chapel, 145–164.
Cotton, Rev. John, 19, 31, 82, 97.
Covenanters, the Scotch, 22.
Coverley, Sir Roger de, 174.
Cradock, George, 175.
Cromwell, Oliver, quoted, 15.
Curtis, Charles Pelham, 64, 104, 136, 151.
Curtis, Charles P., jr., 66.
Curtis, Greely S., 3, 6, 53, 64.
Curtis, the family of, 129.

DALTON, the family of, 151.
Davenport, Rev. Addington, 64, 112.
Deane, Charles, LL.D., letter of Dr. Howe to, 31.
Deblois, Gilbert and Lewis, 175.

Declaration, the, deposing Andros, 42.
Decoration of King's Chapel for 200th Anniversary, 69-72.
Dehon, Theodore, 175.
Dennison, General, 153.
De Tocqueville, quoted, 94.
Diman, Prof. J. Lewis, 185.
Douthit, Rev. Jasper L., letter from, 156.
Dudley, Gov. Joseph, 26, 27, 29, 39, 40, 42, 63, 147; arms of, 62; portrait of, 70, 81, 108.
Dudley, Mrs. Rebecca, portrait of, 70.
Dudley, Thomas, 19.
Dummer, Lieut.-Governor, portrait of, 70, 71.
Dyer, Col. Giles, 173.

ECCLESIASTICAL Commission, the, of King James, 44.
Eckley, Rev. Joseph, ordination of, 101, 107.
Edmands, Miss Gertrude, 66.
Eliot, President Charles William, LL.D., 60, 73, 128; address of, 109.
Eliot, Hon. Samuel Atkins, tribute to, 136.
Elliott, Miss Louise, 66.
Ellis, George Edward, D.D., LL.D., 59; address of, 96.
Ellis, Rufus, D.D., baptism of, 103; description of Early Puritan Worship, quoted from, 18.
Emerson, George Barrell, LL.D., tributes to, 137, 162.
Emerson, Ralph Waldo, quoted, 92.
Emigration, the Great, 35.
Endicott, Hon. William C., letter from, 145.
Endicott, William, 3d, 66.
Episcopal Church, a representative of, 5.
Episcopalian, the modern, 21.
Erving, John, 175.
Escutcheons hung in the church, 62, 71.

Eustis, Gen. Abram, 153.
Everett, Hon. Edward, LL.D., 128.
Everett, Dr. William, original hymn by, 58, 95.

FANEUIL Hall, 86.
Faneuil, Peter, 174; portrait of, 70, 81.
Farley, Frederick Augustus, D.D., 4, 57, 73, 76; letter from, 148-152.
Fenderson, Mrs. E. C., 66.
First Church, 11, 20, 74, 82, 95.
First Church of Salem, 36.
Flags used in the decoration of the church, 62, 70, 71, 72.
"Formes for the servise of the church," 83.
Foote, Rev. Henry Wilder, 5, 6, 53, 58, 64; historical sermons by, on the occasion of the completion of 200 years since the foundation of King's Chapel, 11-52; prayer by 78; address of, 80; closing sermon by, 167-190.
Foxcroft, Francis, 173.
Foxcroft family, arms of the, 62.
Francisca (Shirley), monument of the fair, 132.
Frankland, Sir Harry, 174.
Franklin, Dr. Benjamin, 156.
Franklin, Miss Gertrude, 66.
Freeman, James, D.D., 64, 74, 102, 127, 128, 129, 148, 153, 180; portrait of, 70, 71; preface to King's Chapel prayer-book, quoted, 88; tribute to, 148.
Furness, William H., D.D., letter from, 157.

GAGE, General Thomas, 63.
Gannett, Rev. William C., letter from, 158.
Gardiner, John, 175.
Gardiner, Dr. Sylvester, 175.
Gardner, John L., gift of, 65.
Gedney, Captain, 27, 29.
General Court, the, 27; receive the exemplification of the Charter's condemnation, 27.
George, Captain, 26, 27.

INDEX

George I., King, 174.
George II., King, 85; gift of, 65.
George III., King, gift of, 65.
George, prayer for King, 175.
Gibbins, Dr. John, 174.
Goddard, Dr. C. W., 66.
"God's acre," the earliest, 35.
Gordon, Rev. George Angier, 59; address of, 105.
Gore, Governor, 74; family of, 151.
Gorton, Samuel, 20.
Governor of the Commonwealth of Massachusetts, the, 4, 58, 73.
Governor's pew in King's Chapel, 128; restored, 72.
Great Britain, declaration of peace with, 128; loyalty to, 22.
Green, Samuel S., letter from, 152.
Greenwood, Francis William Pitt, D.D., 64, 74, 87, 149, 151, 154, 162; tributes to, 102, 129, 146, 162; history of King's Chapel by, quoted, 38, 41, 51.
Grew, Edward S., 6, 53.
Guliger, artist, 70.

HACKNEY, tune, 18.
Hall, Thomas B., 6, 53, 64.
Hamilton, Capt. Francis, arms of, 62, 71.
Händel, anthem by, sung, 61; said to have touched the organ, 85.
Harris, Rev. Henry, 64, 173.
Harvard University, the president of, 60; 250th anniversary of, 12; introduction of president of, 108.
Harward, Rev. Thomas, 64, 179.
Haskins, John, 175.
Hatton, Rev. George, 64.
Hawding, Thomas, 175.
Higginson, George, 3, 6, 53, 64.
Hinkley, Governor Thomas, 27.
Hoar, Hon. George Frisbie, letter from, 146.
Holley, Rev. Horace, 131.
Holmes, Oliver Wendell, M.D., LL.D., D.C.L., 5, 61, 73, 127, 130; hymn by, 60; introduction of, 131; poem by, 131.
Homans, Dr. John, 2d, 66.

Horton, Rev. Edward A., letter from, 158.
Hosmer, Rev. Frederic L., letter from, 158.
Howe, Dr. Estes, letter of, 31.
Hull, John, mint-master, 31.
Hunt, Rev. John, 106.
Huntington, Rt. Rev. Frederic D., D.D., letter from, 154.
Hutchinson, Eliakim, 175.
Hutchinson, Gov. Thomas, portrait of, 70, 81.
Hutchinson, Mrs. Anne, 20.

IVERS, James, 175.

JACKSON, Dr. James, 103, 136.
Jackson, Patrick T., 3, 6, 53, 64.
James I., King, 14.
James II., King, 49, 54.
Jekyll, John, 173.
Johonnot, Andrew, 175.
Josselyn, John, 23, 36.
Joyliffe, Mr., pew of, in South Meeting-house, 24.

KEAYNE, Capt. Robert, legacy of, 37.
Kehew, Miss Elene Buffington, 66.
"Kingfisher," ship of war, 71.
King's Chapel, connection of, with the English state, 22; first meeting for organization of, 63; first administration of Lord's Supper, 63; occupancy of South Meeting House, 63; first built of wood, 63; first opened for service, 63; known as Queen's Chapel, 63; present church erected, 63; governors connected with, 63; first service after evacuation of Boston, 63; worshipped with Trinity Church during the Revolution, 63; permitted Old South Church to occupy it, 63; the earliest, 83; liturgy, 63, 86, 102; tributes to, 151, 160; communion service in, 156; library, 178; denominational freedom of, 186.
King's lecturer, the, 101.
King's lecturers, roll of, 64.

INDEX. 197

Kneller, Sir Godfrey, artist, 70, 175.
Knowles, Sir Charles, 85.

LAMB, Horace A., 6, 53.
Lamprell and Marble, decorators, 72.
Lasker, Rev. Raphael, letter from, 159.
Laud, William, Archbishop of Canterbury, 21.
Lechford, Thomas, 23.
Lely, Sir Peter, artist, 70, 173.
"Lethargy," the liturgy so described by Randolph, 41, 97.
Leverett, Governor, wharf of, 43.
Liopoldt, F., artist, 70.
Liturgy of King's Chapel, altered, 63, 180.
Livermore, Abiel Abbot, D.D., letter from, 159.
London, the Bishop of, 38, 43.
Loring, the Misses, portrait belonging to, 62, 71.
Louis XIV., King, 81.
Louisburg, triumph of, 81.
Lowell, A. Lawrence, 6, 53, 64.
Lowell, Francis C., 6, 53.
Lowell, Francis C., tribute to, 137.
Lowell, John Amory, tributes to, 136, 162.
Lyde, Edward, 173.
Lyman, Arthur, 66.
Lyman, Arthur T., 3, 64.
Lyman, Herbert, 66.

MARTINIQUE, disaster of, 81.
Mascarene, the family of, 174.
Mason, Mr., 27, 29, 39.
Massachusetts Bay, banners of, 81.
Massachusetts, commercial independence of, 22.
Massachusetts Historical Society, portraits loaned by, 62, 70; president of, 59, 74; proceedings referred to, 31; rooms of, 95.
Mather, Rev. Cotton, 46.
Mather, Rev. Increase, 45.
Mathers, the, 20, 82.
Mather's "Psalterium Americanum," 59.
May family, 151.

May, Col. Joseph, 73, 129, 175, 176; monument of, 127; gift of, 65.
May, Rev. Joseph, 73, 127; letter from, 160.
May, Rev. Samuel Joseph, 151.
Mayor of Boston, 73.
Meeting-house, use of, to preach in, denied, 29.
Memorial Hall of Harvard College, 29.
Memorial volume authorized, 5.
Minister of King's Chapel, communication from, 3.
Ministers of King's Chapel, roll of, 64.
Ministers, the five Boston, confronting Andros, 45.
Minns, Thomas, 6, 53.
Minot, George R., 6, 53.
Minot, Hon. George Richards, 177.
Minot, George R., Mrs., 62; portrait belonging to family of, 71.
Minot, William, 55; address of welcome, 75; introductions by, 80, 88, 95.
Minot, William, tribute to, 129, 136.
Monument to commemorate the occasion of the Two Hundredth Anniversary of King's Chapel, 5.
Moody, Rev. Joshua, 46.
Morison, John Hopkins, D.D., 60; address of, 122.
Motley, the family of, 151.
Mountfort family, arms of the, 62.
Music, arrangement of, 74.
Myles, Rev. Samuel, 64, 84, 173, 179.

NANTASKET, 26.
Nelson, John, 87, 147, 173.
Newbury, the Second Church in, 59.
New England, His Majesty's territory and dominion of, 54.
New England Historical Genealogical Society, the president of, 147.
New England, polity of, 13, 22, 23.
New Jerusalem Church, First, loan of communion silver to, 161.
New North Church in Boston, communion plate of the, 65.
New South Church, the, 103.

Newton, Thomas, 173.
Nicholson, Sir Francis, 173; arms of, 62, 71.
Northampton, 104, 106.
North, Rev. F. Mason, letter from, 160.
Nowell, Mr. Samuel, prayer of, 27.

O'BRIEN, Mayor, letter from, 145.
Old Church, the, 30.
Old South Church, 20.
Old South Church, expiation to, 86.
Old South Church, minister of, 5, 59, 74.
Oliver, Ebenezer, 177; gift of, 65.
Oliver, the family of, 129.
Orthodox bodies, modification of thought in, 185.
Osgood, Samuel, D.D., gift of, 65.

PADDOCK, Rt. Rev. Benjamin H., D.D., letter from, 154.
Paige, Captain, 26.
Paige, James William, gift of, 65.
Parker, George J., 66.
Parks, Rev. Leighton, letter from, 161.
Paxton, Charles, 175.
Peabody, Andrew Preston, D.D., LL.D., 5, 61, 74; introduction of, 133; address of, 134.
Peabody, Ephraim, D.D., 64, 73, 74, 87; commemorated in address of Dr. Morison, 122; described, 129; tributes to, 122, 129, 147, 159, 162.
Peabody, Prof. Francis Greenwood, 4, 61, 76, 79; introduction of, 134; address of, 138.
Peabody, Robert S., services of, 72.
Pemberton Square, 31.
Pepperell, Sir William, 85.
Perkins, William, 3, 5, 53, 64.
Peter, Rev. Hugh, 36.
Pickering, Edward, tribute to, 137.
Piedmont, massacre in, 28.
Places of worship of King's Chapel, 63.
Playford's "Whole Book of Psalms," 57.

Plummer Professor in Harvard University, the, 61, 138; Emeritus in Harvard University, the, 61, 133, 134.
Portraits, flags, and arms employed in the decoration, 62.
Portraits employed in the decoration, list of, 70.
Port Royal, triumph of, 81.
Pownall, Gov. Thomas, 63; arms of, 62; portrait of, 70.
Pratt, artist, 70.
Pratt, the family of, 151.
Prayer-meetings in King's Chapel, early morning, 156.
"Prayers of ye Church," 83.
President of Harvard College, 4.
Price, Rev. Commissary Roger, 64, 84, 174, 179; arms of, 62; lays corner-stone of Trinity Church, 112; inaugurates services of Trinity Church, 112.
Price, William, 175.
Prison Lane, 30.
Proposed book of Common Prayer, 102.
Proprietors of King's Chapel, annual meeting of, 3.
Protestant Episcopal Church, the, 51, 74, 102.
Protestant Episcopal Diocese of Massachusetts, Right Reverend Bishop of, 111.
Province House, the, 62.
Psalms read in the Commemoration Services, 55, 57, 76.
Psalm, the eighty-fourth, Version of, sung, 57; twenty-third, Version of, sung, 59.
Puritans, the English, 22.
Puritans, the, to be held in honor, 14.
Putnam, Alfred P., D.D., letter from, 163.
Pynchon, Major, 27, 29.

QUAKER, the, 20, 21.
Quebec, triumph of, 81.
Queen's Chapel, the, 63.
Quincy granite, first quarrying of, 84.

INDEX.

RANDOLPH, Edward, 27, 29, 39, 40, 42, 43, 97, 173.
Randolph, Edward, quoted, 21, 24, 25, 26, 40, 44.
Randolph, Mrs., curtesy in prayer-time, 24.
Ratcliffe, Rev. Robert, 25, 26, 28, 29, 30, 36, 37, 39, 48, 64, 82, 173; autograph of, 63.
Read, Hon. John, 174.
Reed, Rev. James, letter from, 161.
Record Book, first page of the earliest, 54.
Remick, H. T., 66.
Revere, John, 3, 64.
Revolution, the, 86, 101.
Reynolds, Sir Joshua, 132.
Rhode Island, a safety-valve, 20.
Richardson, Hon. George C., 64.
"Robison, Esq.," 40.
Robins, Edward B., 66.
Robinson, Gov. George Dexter, LL.D., 58; address of, 89.
Roe, Rev. Stephen, 64.
Roland, the stone, in Bremen, 35, 36.
Roman Catholic King, the representative of, 42.
"Rose" frigate, the, 26.
Roxbury, 31.
Royal Arms from Old Province House, 62, 72.
Royall, the family of, 174.

SACRAMENT, the first, 12, 40, 83.
Salem, 36.
Sampson, Charles E., 6, 53.
Sancroft, William, Archbishop of Canterbury, 44.
Santa Cruz, 104.
Savory and Son, decorators, 72.
Scripture lesson read in Commemoration Services, 76.
Sears, Philip H., 64.
Sears, Richard, 66.
Second Church, the, 20, 82.
Seven Star Lane, 31.
Sewall, Capt. Samuel, house of, 31.
Sewall, Rev. Joseph, 98.

Sewall, Judge, diary of, quoted, 26, 27, 29, 31, 38, 40, 42, 43, 46, 47, 97; his watchfulness over backsliders, 100.
Sherlock, Thomas, Bishop of London, 178.
Shirley, Mrs. Frances, 133.
Shirley, Gov. William, 63, 85, 174, 177; arms of, 62; portrait of, 71.
Shirley, Lieut.-General William, 86.
Shute, Gov. Samuel, 63; arms of, 62.
Smith, Captain, 27.
"Smith, Mr., the joyner," 38.
Smith, Franklin, 151.
Soldier's Monument referred to, 88, 132.
Southack, Cyprian, 173.
Southampton, the Great Emigration sails from, 35.
South Meeting-house, 50, 86; appropriation of, 46, 83, 100, 106; desecration of, 101, 106.
Smybert, artist, 70, 84.
Sprat, Thomas, Bishop of Rochester, 44.
Stanwood, Lemuel, 66.
State House, portrait loaned from, 70.
Stevenson, Hon. Joshua Thomas, tribute to, 137.
Stevenson, Robert H., 64.
Storers, the family of, 129.
Stoughton, Lieut.-Gov. William, 27, 29.
"St. Lawrence," disaster of the, 81.
St. Martyn's, tune, 18.
St. Mary, tune, 18.
St. Paul's day, 47.
St. Thomas, hymn sung to tune of, 95.
Stuart, James, King, 81.
Subscription to build the first King's Chapel, 42.
Sullivan, Rev. Thomas Russell, 151.
Sullivan, Arthur S., anthem by, sung, 61.
Sullivan, Hon. William, LL.D., 128, 151; tribute to, 150.
Summer Street, 31.
Sumner, Hon. Charles, LL.D., funeral of, 157.
Swett, Col. Samuel, 153.

www.ingramcontent.com/pod-product-compliance
Lightning Source LLC
Chambersburg PA
CBHW021355230426
43666CB00006B/532